The Ray Gun Revolution

or, How Ronald Reagan Ruined America

by

Trace Wood

Table of Contents

5	Forward
7	Inauguration
12	Star Wars
21	Founding Fathers
35	The Follow-Up Act
51	The 2nd Founding Fathers
68	The "Socialists"
83	The Main Street Messiah
105	The Burning Bush
116	Well-Intentioned Wolves
126	Bush's Beans
138	Obama
152	Reagan's Trump Card
174	Reversing Course
191	What Happens Now?

Forward

This book was inspired by conversations I had with my family.
Both of my parents were college educated and from the Deep South; my father from a tiny town in Texas called Ben Wheeler, and my mother from a rural community near Okalona, Mississippi. My father served 23 years in the Navy, and saw action in both Korea and Vietnam. If you're doing the math, he left the Navy after Korea, got his college degree, married my mother and taught high school shop in Mississippi for a few years before returning to the Navy for OCS to serve as an officer for the rest of his life. Both he and my mother are interred in Arlington National Cemetery, so honored for that service. Those were the people who raised me. They were also the ones who adopted me.
Almost all of my birth family hail from the West Coast, mostly California. So between my mother's four siblings and their children, my father's brother and his children, my birth mother's brother and his children, and my birth father's *eight* siblings and their children, and my two sisters, one would not be wrong in assuming that I have been exposed to a wide range of opinions along the political spectrum.
Along those same lines, many of my friends have gone in their own directions and have ended up in a wide variety of professions and locations, including some internationally. With the development of social media, it is easier than ever to remain in contact. Their insights have informed my own opinions. I am extremely fortunate to count among my circle NASA engineers, Presidential advisors, professors of economics, journalists, corporate attorneys, Hollywood producers, actors and set designers, doctors, nurses, members of all branches of the military, farmers, teachers and an incredibly wide range of

businessmen from real estate agents to fantasy sports experts. So even if you don't accept that I am at least reasonably knowledgeable about the material covered in this book, the people I've conversed with at length about these topics are. And although at times I might get a little snarky, I have done my best to be as objective as possible.

Something that might be disorienting at first but I hope will make this book more enjoyable is that while I have listed the footnotes at the end of the chapter, I have not numbered any of them. This was done with a purpose. Whenever I read non-fiction, I am both distracted and compelled by footnotes. Once I see that little number, I immediately check out the reference. When I am done, I find myself re-reading the portion that led up to the footnote in an effort to recreate the mood and thoughts I was having while reading the passage the first time. This fits-and-starts approach breaks the flow of the writing/reading and makes it more difficult to focus on the point of the narrative. It's almost as if our conversation is being interrupted by a rude guest who keeps insisting on fact-checking every statement. By eliminating these breaks, our conversation can continue until the natural pause at the end of the chapter. And if you're still curious about the details, the footnotes are right there, in the order in which any controversial points were made. I hope you the reader don't find this method off-putting.

As with any book, there were people who assisted in its creation by giving their own time and energy, providing insights about its crafting and flow. So I'd like to especially thank the contributions of Jocelyn Doherty, Elise and Mike Winneguth, Ron Shandler and Anthony Gibson. I'd also like to add a special thanks to Paul Slansky for his insight and encouragement.

Thank you for reading.

Inauguration

Ask almost anyone living in the United States about Ronald Reagan and they'll pretty consistently tell you that he was a transformative president. The arguments as to whether or not he was great - many from both major party affiliations maintain that he was – are not as uniform, but there is little debate that he significantly changed America.

Since the 1980s there has developed an increasingly wide dovetail in the perception of reality. The very foundations of science and even the most basic facts have become contentious issues. That is troubling enough but the brand of skepticism currently epidemic offers no counter-evidence to warrant those doubts. There is no counterpoint, no discipline, or due diligence to support a robust alternate narrative. The mishmash of conspiracy and magical thinking that fifty years ago would have been dismissed as idiotic drivel and lunacy, is today embraced by an embarrassingly large segment of the population as "thought-provoking" or "controversial".

Given that Reagan was President when this brand of dialectic first gained acceptance, it's reasonable to question whether or not he was somehow responsible for this division we see today. If he was, how much responsibility should we assign to him for it. It also begs the question "Was he great?" And if he wasn't, did he understand what he was promoting? Or was he simply carrying someone else's water?

The starting point for researching this book was the legend itself. Much of the narrative surrounding his legacy didn't make sense. For example, how did Reagan convince the people who pioneered space travel and its central technologies that he was going to build a theoretical space weapon that would not only render their weapons useless but bankrupt their economy if they tried to build a defense against it? How did he revitalize the US economy by reducing taxes on the wealthy by more than 50% while shifting their burden onto everyone else? And what about the debt he created, which increased by 186% over what his predecessor left and has grown by 1962% by presidents who continued his policies? How did he make the world safer? From 1950-1981, the US military engaged in thirty separate actions including two significant wars (Korea and Vietnam). In the 43 years since, that number nearly quadrupled to one hundred ten actions which include three significant wars (two in Iraq and one in Afghanistan). That doesn't sound safer. Before Reagan, terrorism was something people in third-world countries worried about. Since 1981, we have seen two major terrorist attacks on US soil (Oklahoma City and 9/11) and such a proliferation of gun violence that according to the FBI's database, we witness an average of more than one mass shooting every day. Are Americans safer even in their own country? And yet Reagan's politics have been at the center of American policy-making for 40+ years. It just didn't make any sense.

    The problem I encountered in researching this book was that only one side of the story has ever really been told: the side that wants you to believe that Reagan defined what true America is and that he belongs on Mount Rushmore as one of our country's greatest presidents. Rather than rehash the legend, it seemed more useful to present the other side of the equation, an alternative explanation that might better inform the realities we face today, one not built on wistful ideology but answers the questions with evidence, science, and verifiable facts. Where did the embrace of magical conspiracy thinking come from? When did income inequality become an issue? When did people lose the power to influence their representatives? Why is it increasingly difficult for people to realize the American dream that seemed so attainable 50 years ago?

    No doubt you will notice the cover of this book has a picture of Reagan wielding a lightsaber, arguably the most powerful weapon in the Star Wars universe. A competent Jedi could even block and/or deflect incoming blaster fire. But if you look carefully, you'll notice something isn't quite right: one hand has six fingers whereas the other only has four. This image was created by an AI with one line of text as a guideline: "create a portrait of Ronald Reagan with a light saber". The AI knew what both Reagan and a lightsaber looked like, but didn't know that humans have the same number of fingers on both hands. You might also notice that the handle is not straight below his hand and that the light reflection is off-kilter. At first, I thought I'd have to start over but then it dawned on me that this might be the perfect image for this topic: everything looks OK at first glance, but the closer you look, the more discrepancies you find. You might also notice the color of the lightsaber. As you can see by my instructions, I made no request for color, yet any devoted Star Wars fan will recognize which side of The Force this saber represented. Spoiler alert: it wasn't the Rebellion.

The Star Wars theme was chosen with a purpose. SDI, the Strategic Defense Initiative, commonly known as the Star Wars Defense, is often credited for Reagan's greatest acclaimed achievement: bringing down the Soviet Empire. Upon closer inspection, however, it will be clear that the narrative fails the smell test, much like the physics of the fictional Star Wars movie universe. The facts, as you'll see, tell a very different story.

So you're probably saying "So what?! The Soviet Union went down for the count and Reagan was the guy who was in office". Actually, he wasn't. George H. W. Bush was President when the Berlin Wall came down in 1989 and the Soviet Union didn't collapse until 1991. "Who cares if he was the guy who made it happen or not?"

Well, everyone should, because what will be evident is that "achievement" is pretty much the only thing Reagan's legacy is built on. "Rebuilding" the economy was essentially a giveaway to the rich, aided by factors and inertia beyond his control. His domestic agenda, which was hailed as putting America back on its feet turned the US from a creditor nation into a debtor nation, and honestly only one income class truly benefited. That's not exactly putting "America" back on its feet. He opened the doors to the creation of a propaganda machine posing as a news network that has now admitted in depositions that it knowingly spread lies about the integrity of the last presidential election. He deregulated the financial industry to the point where its avarice precipitated three financial meltdowns (and more importantly, three subsequent federal bailouts at taxpayer expense) including one that nearly broke the world's economy (and might still).

During his first inaugural address, he promised that the "longest and worst sustained inflations in our national history would end." He stated that our tax system was holding us back. He complained that we needed to stop deficit spending. He harangued that the government was the problem. He tried to convince the world that Americans were special just because we were Americans and because we were the freest people on Earth. He stated he would reduce the size of the federal government. And he spoke of making a better life for our children and our children's children. He wanted Inauguration Day to be a day of prayer.

None of it was true.

As I'll demonstrate, the Reagan legacy is largely built on falsehoods, myth-making, and half-truths. I'll start with the myths surrounding the Strategic Defense Initiative. In each subsequent chapter, I'll roughly sketch a portion of US history, highlighting presidential policy and how it impacted the development of this country. Then I'll show how Reagan changed it and how his changes continue to affect us. Some of the things I'll detail might sound absolutely crazy. Yet, the facts will demonstrate that as crazy as they sound, the currently accepted explanations make even less sense. In the end, you'll get to decide between the crazy truth and the nonsensical fictions many continue to believe.

With that, let's begin.

US Debt by President
https://www.self.inc/info/us-debt-by-president/

Timeline of US Military Engagements since 1775
https://en.wikipedia.org/wiki/Timeline_of_United_States_military_operations

FBI Crime Data Reporter
https://cde.ucr.cjis.gov/LATEST/webapp/#/pages/home

Star Wars

In 1981, Ronald Reagan signed the National Security Decision Directive (NSDD) 12, which initiated a program to build a strategic anti-ballistic missile defense system, later to become known as the Strategic Defense Initiative (SDI). It became more popularly known as the "Star Wars" defense system. The idea was to prevent Intercontinental Ballistic Missiles (ICBMs) fired from the Soviet Union from ever entering US airspace by shooting them down using a space platform armed with either a powerful laser or microwave gun. It was lauded as a way to win a nuclear conflict that for the previous thirty years had threatened global annihilation. The idea was seeded during a conversation Reagan had with noted physicist Edward Teller, inventor of the hydrogen bomb. Teller told him it should be theoretically possible to achieve, and that it would advent the third generation in the nuclear arms race. When Reagan became President, he was all-in to make it a reality. On March 23, 1983, Reagan announced to the world on live TV that SDI was a go.

In secret, Reagan's advisers had given a copy of the speech to Soviet Ambassador Anatoly Dobrynin to let Russia know he meant business. The ambassador's reply? "You will be opening a new phase to the arms race." Clearly, the Russians understood what Teller had predicted. Reagan countered that when the US developed this system, as a show of his goodwill and to prove his claim that he wanted to rid the world of the threat of nuclear weapons, he would share the technology with the Soviets.

The Soviets knew better: Reagan was offering smoke, mirrors, and nonsense. Among his detractors this fantasy earned him the nickname "Ronald RayGun".

To this day, more than 40 years later, science has yet to develop a laser powerful enough to take down an ICBM. Lockheed Martin projects that later this decade, they will eventually succeed in constructing a 1000-kilowatt laser. That would be powerful enough to take down a missile but it wouldn't be like a Star Wars blaster which blows the target up the instant the bolt hits. It'd be more like heating water in your electric kettle. However, so far they've only managed to construct one capable of generating 300 kilowatts. So, not close.

Reagan's space ray gun would conceivably disable some function of the missile, either the propulsion, guidance, or even the warhead itself. The time from a silo launch is detected to its target is between 22-26 minutes, less if it's launched from a submarine. Ideally, the platform would intercept and disable the missiles in the boost and post-boost phases, before they reach apex altitude, which only gives it a few minutes to disable its target. Anything beyond that might still result in the materials reaching US soil. Since some of them would have multiple warheads, the most lethal would need to be targeted first which requires means identifying them on the fly. Ground-based lasers would then be used to minimize the number of casualties by destroying or disabling any missiles that made it through. They wouldn't eliminate casualties; just lessen the damage.

In 1989, the Department of Defense announced they had launched a particle beam weapon into space, ran tests for four minutes, and brought it back to Earth. But they never announced what the tests entailed. For all we know, they launched a flashlight into low Earth orbit, turned it on and off for four minutes, and brought it safely back to Earth. The light from a flashlight qualifies as a particle beam (since light is both particle and wave) and the military is well-known for exaggerating capability to secure further funding. Just look at the seventeen years it took them to finally bring the Bradley fighting vehicle online, or the F-35 multi-purpose fighter which is well over budget already. That program, begun in 1995 with a prototype first flying in 2000, is scheduled to build roughly 1400 planes for a total cost of around $1.5 trillion. Until a few years ago, the plane could not fire its guns while flying or operate when it was raining. It is not unreasonable to assume that what they staged in 1989 was nothing more than a press release.

According to Popular Mechanics: "There are a lot of technical issues that need to be resolved to make space-based particle beams work. The neutral particle beam will need to hold a coherent beam over the 1,000 kilometers or so (roughly 650 miles) from low-earth orbit to the ground. The system will need a sufficiently portable power supply. The Pentagon will need to figure out how to detect a launching missile, pass the data to a satellite, and then have that satellite engage the missile. It will also have to figure out how many satellites it will need, and since objects in low-earth orbit do not remain stationary, will need a fleet of satellites to ensure that one or more will be over the target in the event of a launch. These are all issues Washington wrestled with in the 1980s—and then failed to deploy a usable system. Only time will tell if things are different this time around." It seems that time has already told.

The scale of an attack is also problematic. It is hard enough to target a single object traveling at 15,000 miles per hour, let alone the thousands that would be launched in either an attack or a counterattack from positions around the globe. Land-launched ICBMs have a range of 7500 miles. The Soviets, with their fleet of nuclear attack submarines, could also effectively launch missiles from the seas within a 3000-mile range of the 95,471-mile-long US coastline. When Reagan was in office the Soviets had roughly 1400 ICBM launch silos, more than 60 submarines carrying a total of more than 900 ICBMs, and several thousand more that could be launched from mobile missile carriers. Assuming the space ray gun could destroy one missile every second, the system would still need many active platforms in a position to intercept them all in time. Currently, 31 satellites in space provide GPS coordinates, but only 24 are necessary for them to be effective. A GPS server needs four satellites to pinpoint one location in three dimensions, but their signals can travel thousands of miles. Because of the limited range of each space ray, SDI would need four times as many satellites to defeat an attack.

If that's not enough to solve, nearly everything we put in space has been built by private contractors, largely funded by government agencies. Even SpaceX has a huge contract with NASA. Many of these projects are built by the lowest bidder, which means occasional snafus occur, like sending up the Hubble telescope with a defective mirror. Within minutes, such a malfunction would see Denver, Las Vegas, and Pensacola all erased from the map.

It didn't matter.

The Soviets knew Reagan was bluffing. They were, after all, the people who had invented space travel and exploration. In 1903, Konstantin Tsolkovsky calculated the necessary speeds for orbits around the Earth as well as travel to the moon via multi-stage rockets powered by liquid oxygen and liquid hydrogen. He didn't just fantasize about traveling to the moon like Jules Verne had in his 1865 novel From the Earth to the Moon. He had worked out the math and physics necessary to accomplish it and had the basic design for a spaceship to do it. That means the same year a couple of bicycle repairmen from Ohio were credited with inventing powered flight, Tsolkovsky had figured out how to go to the moon. The Soviets had been the first to put an object into orbit (Sputnik), an animal into orbit (a dog named Laika), the first to put animals into orbit and safely return them to Earth (Belka and Strelka), put both a man (Yuri Gagarin) and a woman (Valentina Tereshkova) in orbit, the first to walk in space (Alexei Leonov), the first to land a first remote-controlled robot on the moon (Lunakhod 1, which by the way, was the template for the first Mars rovers), and until the International Space Station (much of which was built in Russia) came along, held the record for the longest stays in space aboard Salyut, Almaz and Mir space stations. The only thing they didn't win was the race to land the first humans on the moon. That's a big miss considering that putting humans on the moon and returning them safely home was and still is the greatest scientific and engineering achievement in the history of mankind. They were far more concerned with the possibility that the US would use the bluff as a guise to develop a space-based ICBM platform from which to launch an offensive attack.

If you think the Russians were paranoid, remember that during the American era (1776 - present) there have been two empires hell-bent on expansion in Europe (France under Napoleon and Germany under Hitler), and both of them invaded Russia. If you want to go back further, Russia has been invaded by Sweden, Poland, Turkey (the Ottomans), and even the Mongols. During their own civil war in 1917, the US sent troops to Russia to help the czarists, so they had every reason to distrust the West, especially the US.

At their historic meeting in Reykjavik, Iceland, Reagan purportedly offered the technology to Gorbachev as part of a disarmament agreement, to which Gorbachev replied, "I do not take your idea of sharing SDI seriously. You don't want to share even petroleum equipment, automatic machine tools, or equipment for dairies while sharing SDI would be a second American revolution—and revolutions do not occur all that often."

The reality, which is backed by all of the available information obtained from Soviet labs and research facilities after the Fall, was that they merely started looking into ways to defeat SDI. It turns out that costs less than a tenth of what "Star Wars" would have cost had it been implemented. For example, lasers are easily defended against using mirrors or other reflective surfaces. Once they figured that out, they simply went about business as usual. The topic of why the Soviet Union actually fell will be addressed in a later chapter.

During the November 1985 Geneva Summit, there was a moment when President Ronald Reagan and Soviet Premier Mikhail Gorbachev paused their negotiations and went for a walk. Only their personal interpreters were present during this private conversation, and for many years, the content of their discussion was shrouded in secrecy, hidden from both the American and Russian public. However, in a 2009 interview with Charlie Rose and Ronald Reagan's Secretary of State George Schultz, Gorbachev disclosed a surprising revelation. He shared that during their walk, Reagan had asked him straightforwardly if they could put aside their differences in the event that an alien invasion threatened the world. Gorbachev was nonplussed, unsure whether the American President was actually serious or making a joke.

Reagan was very familiar with the "Day the Earth Stood Still" (1951), the original "War of the Worlds" (radio in 1938, movie in 1953), "Close Encounters of the Third Kind" (1977), and the 1975 news story that later inspired the movie "Fire in the Sky" (1993). He had even read a report sent to him by the Citizens Advisory Council on National Space Policy, an ad hoc weekend consortium of conservative-minded sci-fi writers, engineers, and aerospace professionals (including four former astronauts) who offered proposals for America's future in space. That said, no credible authority would ever put the threat of alien invasion above the possibility of nuclear annihilation. Yet to Reagan, it was a very real possibility. His defenders will try to reframe this as Reagan seeking a way to negotiate, a way of finding common ground, but the simplest explanation is that he was more afraid of invasion from extraterrestrials than he was of nuclear war.

Those were not isolated occasions when Reagan got his policy ideas from movies. He firmly believed that the US could win a nuclear exchange, albeit with acceptable casualties. But in 1983 that changed. So what changed his mind? Was it the September 26, 1983, close call when Soviet radar falsely detected a nuclear launch that nearly triggered an all-out reprisal? A duty officer named Stanislav Petrov was stationed at his radar console when it detected an incoming flight of five ICBMs heading toward Moscow. The US Navy had held an exercise earlier that year in which planes intentionally overflew Soviet air space. Was that simply testing the waters for an attack? But why would they only launch five missiles? No doubt had they known what was happening, the Russian high command would have ordered an all-out counterattack. Instead of notifying his superiors, though, Petrov checked with other radar operators. They saw no signs of an attack. He rightly dismissed it as a glitch and did not report his findings until later. It turned out to be an atmospheric event that registered as incoming missiles on his radar screen. But rather than being hailed as a hero for averting what would have certainly been mutually assured destruction of not only both countries but most of the planet, he was reprimanded for "mistakes in his log book". That event wasn't known to the press until a decade later, but certainly word of that near-catastrophic snafu would have reached Reagan within days. Did he have a Damascus road moment and suddenly realize the folly of nuclear brinksmanship from such a close call? Of course not. What about the numerous published policy papers that stated nuclear war, even limited in scope, would be catastrophic? Who are you kidding?

    It wasn't until he watched the TV movie "The Day After" in October of that year that he came to the realization that nuclear war might be really bad. In June of that same year, he had also watched "Wargames". He was alarmed by how easy it looked to hack into the defense computers to initiate such a conflict. When told the movie had actually undersold how vulnerable our defense systems were to hacking, it was reported that he was depressed for a day. Two years later in Geneva, for the first time during his presidency, Reagan met with Gorbachev face-to-face. Their landmark meeting in Reykyavik to agree to a reduction in nuclear arms took place less than a year later in October 1986. And to this day, Matthew Broderick still hasn't been awarded the Presidential Medal of Freedom. Acting can be such a thankless job.

So why exactly did the Soviet Union fall? Was Reagan the first to knowingly tell titanic lies? Or did he even know what was and wasn't technologically possible? Did he understand any of it, or was he just a willing tool for the people he had associated with for his entire political career? Perhaps to better answer those questions, we should start at the beginning.

History of SDI
https://ahf.nuclearmuseum.org/ahf/history/strategic-defense-initiative-sdi/

The Pentagon Wants to Test a Space-Based 'Particle Beam' by 2023
https://www.popularmechanics.com/military/weapons/a26858944/pentagon-particle-beam-space-2023/

THE WHY, WHAT, AND HOW OF THE STRATEGIC DEFENSE INITIATIVE
https://apps.dtic.mil/sti/pdfs/ADA346048.pdf

Nuclear U.S. and Soviet/Russian Intercontinental Ballistic Missiles, 1959-2008
https://journals.sagepub.com/doi/full/10.2968/065001008

History of the Bradley Fighting Vehicle
https://user.eng.umd.edu/~austin/enes489p/lecture-resources/BradleyFightingVehicle-Scenario.pdf

Issues with the F-35
https://www.defensenews.com/smr/hidden-troubles-f35/

https://www.defensenews.com/air/2023/06/12/pentagon-to-halt-upgraded-f-35-deliveries-in-july-amid-software-woes/

https://www.defensenews.com/smr/hidden-troubles-f35/2021/07/16/the-number-of-major-f-35-flaws-is-shrinking-but-the-pentagon-is-keeping-details-of-the-problems-under-wraps/

https://www.forbes.com/sites/davidaxe/2021/02/25/after-20-years-the-f-35-stealth-fighter-is-still-stuck-in-testing/?sh=397d83d09b2c

https://nationalpost.com/news/national/defence-watch/f-35-unable-to-fire-its-gun-because-of-software-issues

How Sci-Fi Like 'WarGames' Led to Real Policy During the Reagan Administration
https://www.newamerica.org/weekly/how-sci-fi-wargames-led-real-policy-during-reagan-administration/

Dark Territory review – how WarGames and Reagan shaped US cyberwar battle https://www.theguardian.com/technology/2016/mar/20/dark-territory-review-ronald-reagan-matthew-broderick-war-games-american-cyberwar

This TV Movie About Nuclear War Depressed Ronald Reagan
https://medium.com/war-is-boring/this-tv-movie-about-nuclear-war-depressed-ronald-reagan-fb4c25a50044

Reagan and Gorbachev Agreed to Pause the Cold War in Case of an Alien Invasion
https://www.smithsonianmag.com/smart-news/reagan-and-gorbachev-agreed-pause-cold-war-case-alien-invasion-180957402/

The Founding Fathers

Obviously, Ronald Reagan was not the first President of our country to sell an empty bill of goods. In fact, the country was practically founded on it.

"All men are created equal"?

While it is still possible we will eventually achieve that ideal, it is evident from the events of the last ten years (ten? OK, the last 250) that we haven't reached it. From the disproportionate number of fatal incidents and incarcerations for indigenous peoples and people of color to the degree and frequency of felonious behavior committed by the wealthy and privileged yet still escaping punishment, it is glaringly evident that all men are not viewed as equals under the law. That's even before we get into the imbalances between men and women. So voluminous is the evidence that to suggest it is only one mountain grossly undersells it. It is more like a mountain range that extends over an entire continent.

Honestly, it's questionable whether the Founding Fathers even meant it. They may have believed it among their peers as they discussed ways to separate from Great Britain, but it's pretty clear that they didn't view non-property holders (particularly slaves) as equals. They did recognize, however, that to get the common man to fight a war to lower their taxes to zero they would have to come up with a really good slogan and some ideas that would get people excited enough to put their lives on the line for a benefit they would never live to see.

If that sounds cynical, consider that 34 of the 47 men depicted in Turnbull's famous painting of the signing of the Declaration of Independence were slaveholders: Josiah Bartlett,

Charles Carroll, Samuel Chase, Abraham Clark, George Clinton, John Dickinson, William Floyd, Benjamin Franklin, John Hancock, Benjamin Harrison, Joseph Hewes, Thomas Heyward Jr., William Hooper, Stephen Hopkins, Francis Hopkinson, Thomas Jefferson, Richard Henry Lee, Francis Lewis, Philip Livingston, Robert R. Livingston, Thomas Lynch, Arthur Middleton, Lewis Morris, Robert Morris, William Paca, George Read, Benjamin Rush, Edward Rutledge, Richard Stockton, William Whipple, Thomas Willing, John Witherspoon, Oliver Wolcott and George Wythe all at one point or another (and most for their lives) owned slaves. Granted, there were actually fifty-five attendees of the Conventions, and not all of the ones who were pictured in the Turnbull painting were actually there, but the ratio is revealing about the composition of the people running the country when it began. That ratio would have been even higher had Georgia bothered to send representatives to the first two Continental Congresses. In fact, until the 1830s, half of Congress was comprised of slaveholders, and it wasn't until the Civil War that the percentage dropped below 40%. Even after it had been made illegal, people were still electing former slaveholders to represent them. As late as 1880, 20% of the membership in Congress were former slaveholders, and it wasn't until the 1920s that the number dropped to zero.

    The other thirteen of the signers, by the way, would all fall under the category of the top 1% by today's standards: John Adams, Samuel Adams, George Clymer, William Ellery, Elbridge Gerry, Samuel Huntington, Thomas McKean, Robert Treat Paine, Roger Sherman, Charles Thomson, George Walton, William Williams, and James Willson. All this to say is that when they wrote about all men being equal, they were only talking about themselves and not the other 98-99% of the population.

    Want more privilege? Only six of the signers of the Declaration of Independence also signed the Constitution: George Clymer, George Read, Roger Sherman, Robert Morris, James Willson, and Benjamin Franklin. Only six of the men who had so passionately argued for independence, who were so eager to start a new country that 'protected the rights of the people' bothered to stick around to make the laws. For the rest, as long as they didn't have to pay taxes, they were fine with whatever the others came up with.

In fact, if you go down the list of signers, much like the people who represent us currently in Congress, very few were what we might today call "good people". One would be very hard-pressed to suggest that their efforts were altruistic. But they knew that they couldn't exactly write, "We the rich white guys of America, want to start a country in which we get all the rights and all the money".

So they made promises like freedom of religion. That was certainly a good one but it wasn't as if the crown was actively arresting colonials for not venerating King George III as the pope. There were many brands of Christianity being practiced. It's doubtful any of the Founders ever considered the possibility that representatives and leaders in America might one day worship Allah, Rama, Buddha, Satan, or no one at all. They regarded those who did as "savages". They did, however, have more than a passing knowledge of people who didn't believe in the Christian God. Many of them were deists, which is to say they believed in a higher power but didn't think anyone could speak on his/her/its behalf. Thomas Jefferson, one of the more outspoken deists, even edited his own version of the Bible called "The Life and Morals of Jesus" by literally cutting and pasting the passages he thought relevant. As a testament to his beliefs, the text excludes all the miracles and supernatural references.

Freedom of speech was another big one. Freedom of the Press was another. They put those first for a reason. It was important to be able to express oneself, even if it meant thumbing one's nose at authority. What's interesting is that several of the Founders thought it was a good idea for everyone else, but not so great when they were the subject of that free speech. For example, John Adams passed the Alien and Sedition Acts which made it illegal to oppose the government on matters of foreign affairs. A couple of people were even sentenced to prison for making personal allegations about Adams and then-VP Thomas Jefferson.

Maybe the biggest "right" was the right to be free from warrantless searches and seizures, which, oddly enough, is still something that routinely gets infringed upon today.

The rest of the documents they wrote were pretty much declarations of freedoms they themselves wanted but did not necessarily think everyone else should have. The right to vote, if you'll remember, was restricted to the "consent of the governed", otherwise known as the white male landowners who made up about 2% of the population.

There is one misconception, however, where Reagan significantly differs from the Founders: the United States was never a "Christian nation". The Founding Fathers were pretty tired of people telling them what to believe and certainly weren't in the mood to create another England. One fake pope (whose office was created because divorce was considered worse than having a bastard son) was enough. Ironically, that turned out to be irrelevant because Henry VIII divorced, murdered, and annulled six wives yet still didn't get a son. The even greater irony is that one of the kids he fathered, Elizabeth 1, turned into one of the most effective leaders the world has ever seen. That alone should have made it clear to men everywhere to never underestimate women, but four centuries later we're still pretty stupid that way.

The Founding Fathers wanted to create a secular nation that at its heart had principles they were familiar with (what many people call "Christian" but are implicitly humanitarian and were actually very similar to the Articles of the Iroquois Confederacy) without all the Catholic/Anglican/Protestant Church nonsense. I'm not going to quote all the times they wrote explicitly these very thoughts because there are literally volumes of books that provide both the quotes and the context in which they were penned. Another mountain range of them, actually. But there is one by our 4th President and primary author of the Constitution, James Madison, that gets right to the point:

"The purpose of separation of church and state is to keep forever from these shores the ceaseless strife that has soaked the soil of Europe in blood for centuries."

Or this one from our 2nd President, John Adams:

"The government of the United States is not, in any sense, founded on the Christian religion."

Thomas Jefferson was quoted as saying, "Christianity neither is nor ever was a part of the common law," which doesn't require much interpretation to mean that he wasn't in favor of the Bible ever being used to support the Constitution.

Most of the founders and signers did indeed fall into one of the many Christian traditions – Anglican, Presbyterian, Congregationalist, Quaker, Lutheran, Roman Catholic, and Dutch Reformed. However, it is incredibly problematic to try to appoint any one of those belief systems as the primary guiding principle of our founding documents, any more than the Code of Hammurabi, which predated Christianity by 1700 years, or the Gortyn Code which precedes it by 400 years. Even the Corpus Juris Civillus (AD 529) and the Iroquois Confederacy of Nations (initiated in AD 1450) have more in common with our founding documents than the Bible.

These men had no intention of creating a Christian nation. It was difficult enough for fifty or so landowners to agree on whether or not the country should even allow political parties. The Venn diagram that eventually became the Constitution was about as bare bones a document as they could agree on. These men were extremely self-interested, much like the upper classes are today, and their sense of morality only went as far as their own fingers.

Ben Franklin, for example, was essentially the Rupert Murdoch of his day. His paper, Poor Richard's Almanac, was a tabloid full of fictions and gossip. There was hardly anything newsworthy about it. He was a serial flirt, likely a philanderer and had pornographic sketches drawn of him with the ladies. There's evidence he didn't invent some of the things he is often credited with like bifocals and the lightning rod. There's also strong evidence – in the form of more than a dozen skeletons found in his basement - that he bought cadavers illegally to perform dissections. And despite being a member of the Abolitionist's Society (as was James Madison), he owned slaves. Smart, intellectually curious, charming... yes, all of those in spades. Principled? Absolutely not.

Well known is the fact that Thomas Jefferson owned slaves. Although, unlike the other Founders, we have genetic proof he had sex with his. He hated the idea of a federal government, instead arguing that the states should have autonomy to do whatever they wanted. In doing so, he clearly wasn't considering the benefits of a national currency, or how badly currency manipulation could ravage a fledgling economy. We know he didn't understand how money worked or how it could be exploited because he died broke. Actually, converting to 2023 dollars, he was more than $2.4 million in debt when he died according to his son, despite having all the benefits of plantation wealth his entire life. When his family sold Monticello, along with all of his possessions (his furniture, farm equipment, personal belongings, 1000 acres of land, and 130 slaves), they were still only able to pay about 20% of his debt. Much of his estate was sold to a pharmacist named James Barclay who not only hated Jefferson but wanted to convert all of his land into a silkworm farm. He destroyed the gardens and the orchards Jefferson had planted but ended up going belly up, selling the place just six years later for one-third the price he paid for it. Imagine hating someone so much that you destroy yourself in the process of trying to dismantle everything they had accomplished... kinda like Donald Trump tried to do with the

Obama legacy. Well, I guess you don't have to imagine much. Thankfully, Barclay never ran for President.

Our first president, George Washington, was also a slave owner. At the end of the Revolution and as the government was just forming in Philadelphia, he rotated his slaves back home every few months to Mount Vernon because in 1780 the state had passed the Gradual Abolition Act. That law freed slaves after six months of residence in the state. It was based on the Quaker belief – Pennsylvania was founded by William Penn, a Quaker – that slavery was immoral. They had come to that conclusion in the 1600s. Washington, however, with help from Martha, couldn't just let them become freed. That would mean they'd have to buy new ones which could get very expensive, even if they bought them in bulk. To date, the largest single auction block of slaves in America ever uncovered was 600 people, but sales of dozens at a time were not uncommon. The less well-publicized feature of slavery was, like any asset, that slaves could be used as collateral for loans. There's an old banking aphorism: let your money work for you. Well, slavery was quite literally that. But it's not as if Washington had to worry too much about money; by modern estimations, Washington was our 3rd richest president, coming in at close to $600 million in net worth in today's dollars. His presidential salary ($25,000, which is equivalent to nearly $900,000 today) was 2% of our national budget. You might ask "How did he make his money?" By marrying into it (Martha was rich from a previous marriage) and by running one of the biggest whiskey operations in America. This makes Washington seem a lot more like our contemporary politicians, doesn't it? But wait, there's more!

The story about his famous teeth being made of wood? That was nonsense. They were actually made from both hippopotamus teeth and – wait for it - those of his slaves. There's still some debate as to whether he waited until they were dead to remove them. Some will laud him for actually freeing his slaves, but he did not do so until after his death, which forced his wife (who actually owned more) to release hers out of fear for her life that they might cause an uprising. That begs the question: why would she fear this if her husband had been such a good man? If he was anything like his grandson-in-law, Robert E. Lee, she had plenty to fear. Also, since Virginia was still a slave state, unless she also helped her former slaves escape to an emancipated state – the nearest one being Pennsylvania – they would likely be rounded up and sold into servitude again. Not exactly the flex of saintliness his apologists were hoping for.

He was probably responsible for starting the French-Indian War. Not that France and England were ever best buddies, but on a routine scouting mission and wanting to prove his worthiness for higher command, he summarily executed a French diplomat after accusing him of being a spy (albeit with no evidence). That single incident sparked the war. That same ambition netted him six losses out of nine engagements against the British during our War for Independence.

That's not to say that he didn't have any virtues. The aforementioned character stains are just a counterbalance to the narrative that he and his fellow Founders were infallible men of great wisdom. They absolutely were not. They were just men, subject to the same biases, passions, and ignorance that everyone is. For all his glaring flaws as a man and as a leader, there are some things Washington should be given great credit for, like understanding the importance of intelligence in war. He coordinated the Culper Spy ring, which was a decisive factor in determining the outcome of the Revolution. The intelligence his network gathered was instrumental in putting resources in play where they would most effectively further the cause. It also can not be overstated how important it was for him to step away from the Presidency after two terms. That single act assured that there would never be a king of the United States (as long as Donald Trump never wins the office again). So even though he was completely fed up with all the infighting and politicking of running the show, walking away from such immense power is never as easy as dropping a microphone.

So how does this tie to Reagan?

Washington had more than his fair share of self-important drama. For example, he once wrote: "We must assert our rights, or submit to every imposition that can be heaped upon us; till custom and use, will make us as tame, and abject slaves, as the blacks we rule over with such arbitrary sway", comparing his taxation from the king to slavery. Sounds more like Reagan's libertarian tax policy advisor Grover Norquist than the "sensible" founder we commemorate each year with a holiday. Funny, but I don't remember King George ever extracting any of Washington's teeth for his own personal use. By the way, the British actually granted freedom to any slave who left his/her revolutionary master. Eventually, some of the northern colonies followed suit for fear that the slaves would form a formidable army against their cause, although that didn't stop the northern banks from financing the trade. It's an interesting twist because the slave trade wasn't outlawed in Britain until 1807, and slavery itself wasn't abolished there until 1833. England granted rights to people in the colonies that they hadn't given in their own country, the exact opposite of the King's view on taxation.

Washington himself stated after the war that he regretted owning slaves but that the only way to abolish the practice was through legislation. That is an extremely important and revealing stand. Slavery, owning another human being as chattel, is one of the most evil sins perpetrated on mankind. Here is Washington, the "father of our country", fully admitting that he, one of the wealthiest landowners in the country, could not simply free his slaves. Others would have to do it, too. The only way to get men of his ilk and standing to do what was obviously right was to involve the government. In fact, the government had to make a law prohibiting the behavior that any rational person would deem abhorrent. And it wasn't just Washington who was unwilling to do the right thing. Thomas Jefferson, James Madison, Ben Franklin,

James Monroe, Patrick Henry, John Hancock, and even Alexander Hamilton all wrote it was morally wrong but could not bring themselves to do anything about it, even when they had the power of legislation to do it. The leaders of industry always blanch against regulating their behavior, yet the founders of our country understood that they could not help themselves from doing immoral acts unless the government stepped in.

And this is how it applies to Ronald Reagan. He openly railed against government intrusion. He insisted in his speeches that the government was a necessary evil. However, his actual policies told a very different story. About the only places where his actions followed his words were in the deregulation of business and the reduction of taxes on the wealthy. Unfortunately, that was where government regulation was most needed. Human behavior has not changed radically in the last 300 years. If the richest men in the world back then couldn't govern their appetites without laws regulating them, there is no reason why they would now. There is an obvious need for laws and enforcement. These highly revered men admitted they knew what they were doing was wrong and to a man stated that the only way they'd stop was if the government stopped them. That should be everything you need to know. When something is clearly immoral, there should not be a sense of "well he's doing it, too, so it can't be that bad". No, the correct response is "That's wrong, and even if I as an individual don't have the power to stop it, at least my government does." Good government plays a role in maintaining the health and welfare of ALL of its constituents, not just the ones who give the most political contributions.

In addition, for the rule of law to be the supreme guide as the Founders intended, government *must* be free of the entanglements of religion. The practice of slavery is mentioned quite a bit in the Bible with little comment as to its morality. That alone should disqualify it as a founding principle for this country. To be clear, the notion that the US is or was always a Christian nation is a fiction created by Reagan. I'm sure some of you are saying, "Hey, Reagan didn't put God in our political vocabulary. Presidents have been closing their speeches with 'and may God bless America' since the invention of broadcast media."

Actually, they haven't. If you look back, Lyndon Johnson's "I will not seek another term" speech was the first to close with "and may God bless you all." Nixon closed one of his speeches regarding the Watergate scandal with "God bless America". That's it. Twice in the history of 20th-century presidential speeches before Reagan. And if you think about it, there have been some pretty incredibly important speeches in the last century: Carter's "malaise" speech (and the evidence is pretty compelling that he was the only practicing Christian in the Oval Office in the last 75 years), Nixon's resignation, Kennedy's "Cuban missile crisis" speech, Eisenhower's "military-industrial complex" farewell, Truman dropping the atom bomb, and numerous FDR fireside chats during World War 2… none of them closed with "and may God bless America." In fact, many of the speeches don't even mention God, even during the most desperate times. Yet somehow America made it through. Reagan, on the other hand, ended every speech with that regardless of how banal or serious to topic was. Ever since, every president has done the same. Why? Was Reagan somehow moved by the spirit? That's a highly dubious position since he rarely attended church.

Do you know what else the other presidents didn't do? Hire advisors from extreme religious groups like Moral Majority's Executive Director Robert Billings (who was later named Secretary of Education under Reagan) to help with their campaigns to court the evangelical right. They also didn't platform extreme religious groups at their nominating convention, as Reagan did in 1980, or ask to "lead a silent prayer" during their acceptance speeches. Nor did they elevate the profiles of religious carnival barkers like Pat Robertson or Jerry Falwell. Reagan leaned into it because he knew it provided him a rabid political base, one that would not ask questions as long as he pushed the right button for one-issue voters. He was also the only president to declare a "year of the Bible" (1983), and the only one to issue an official alert to suggest ways for school administrators to introduce prayer in public schools.

Of the three books Reagan most cited as influential in his life, the one he drew from most often when he went off script during his speeches was a testimonial written by Whittaker Chambers, the man who had been the primary prosecution witness against Alger Hiss during the HUAC (House UnAmerican Committee) trials. Reagan himself had used his position as president of the Screen Actors Guild to secretly inform the committee about suspected communists in Hollywood. Chambers, a born-again Christian, was initially portrayed as a whistle-blower accusing Hiss of being a communist by Senator Joe McCarthy and his wingman, the junior congressman from California, Richard Nixon. However, Hiss was not convicted of the primary charges brought against him. Instead, he was convicted on a charge of perjury. What was he caught lying about? Knowing Whittaker Chambers. The most interesting aspect, though, was that to prove that Hiss had known him, Chambers was forced by opposing counsel to provide evidence in the form of microfilm, letters, and papers. That evidence proved that he too had committed perjury during his testimony. It also revealed that Chambers had been just as active a participant in Hiss's activities. Ironically, the Chambers book that Reagan so loved was named for a person who is supposed to tell the truth no matter the consequences: Witness.

The Founding Fathers Views of Slavery
https://www.battlefields.org/learn/articles/founding-fathers-views-slavery

Founding Fathers and Slaveholders
https://www.smithsonianmag.com/history/founding-fathers-and-slaveholders-72262393/

The Founding Fathers and Slavery
https://www.britannica.com/topic/The-Founding-Fathers-and-Slavery-1269536

List of Founding Fathers Who Owned Slaves
https://www.historyoasis.com/post/founding-fathers-who-owned-slaves

The Founding Fathers, Deism, and Christianity
https://www.britannica.com/topic/The-Founding-Fathers-Deism-and-Christianity-1272214

The Founding Fathers Feared Political Factions Would Tear the Nation Apart
https://www.history.com/news/founding-fathers-political-parties-opinion

List of Presidents Who Owned Slaves
https://en.wikipedia.org/wiki/List_of_presidents_of_the_United_States_who_owned_slaves

More than 1,800 congressmen once enslaved Black people. This is who they were, and how they shaped the nation.
https://www.washingtonpost.com/history/interactive/2022/congress-slaveowners-names-list/

Ben Franklin
https://www.phillymag.com/news/benjamin-franklin-facts/

https://allthingsliberty.com/2016/06/benjamin-franklins-battery-of-lovers/

History of Bifocals
https://web.archive.org/web/20110613044912/http://www.college-optometrists.org/en/knowledge-centre/museyeum/online_exhibitions/artgallery/bifocals.cfm

The European Franklin
https://www.jstor.org/stable/227388

Sale of Monticello
https://www.monticello.org/research-education/thomas-jefferson-encyclopedia/sale-monticello/

George Washington
https://www.mountvernon.org/george-washington/health/washingtons-teeth/george-washington-and-slave-teeth/

https://www.smithsonianmag.com/history/george-washington-whiskey-businessman-180951364/

https://www.mountvernon.org/george-washington/french-indian-war/washington-and-the-french-indian-war/

George Washington Used Legal Loopholes to Avoid Freeing His Slaves
https://www.smithsonianmag.com/smart-news/george-washington-used-legal-loopholes-avoid-freeing-his-slaves-180954283/

Let's Get Real about Robert E. Lee and Slavery
https://www.washingtonpost.com/history/2021/09/10/robert-e-lee-slavery/

How Banks Played a Role in Upholding Slavery During the 19th Century
https://gwtoday.gwu.edu/how-banks-played-role-upholding-slavery-during-19th-century

How slavery became America's first big business
https://www.vox.com/identities/2019/8/16/20806069/slavery-economy-capitalism-violence-cotton-edward-baptist

The evangelical presidency: Reagan's dangerous love affair with the Christian right
https://www.salon.com/2014/05/18/the_evangelical_presidency_reagans_dangerous_love_affair_with_the_christian_right/

The Intellectual Origins of Ronald Reagan's Faith
https://www.heritage.org/political-process/report/the-intellectual-origins-ronald-reagans-faith

The Follow-up Act

The framework of the United States we recognize today coalesced over the next hundred years, from a libertarian's wet dream through a bloody civil war that still reverberates into a nation powerful enough to rise above the challenges of the 20th century.

It began after the last of the Continental Founding Presidents left office. After Adams, Jefferson, Madison, Monroe, and to a certain extent Quincy Adams, (whose father had been president and who had served under two others) that we get into the wilderness that extended beyond the vision of the signers of the Declaration of Independence. That's when we get Andrew Jackson.

Like most populist politicians, Jackson came from humble beginnings. Born poor, he did well for himself through his law practice and his adventuring. He spent much of his lawyering days collecting debts for creditors and seizing property where warranted. Isn't it strange how populists so often claim to be a "man of the people" but they almost always make their fortunes screwing those same people over? Anyway, he believed in the axiom that "an ounce of justice was worth more than a pound of law", and unfortunately for those who crossed him, his idea of justice was often self-interested.

For example, in one particular case during his early years as a prosecutor, he was getting his ass handed to him at every turn by a well-known, highly esteemed lawyer. Desperate not to lose while simultaneously being exposed as the unprepared, under-educated hack that he was, he simply challenged opposing counsel in court to a duel, claiming that he had been slandered. Jackson's motto should have been, "If you can't beat him, shoot him." Later, he served on the Tennessee Supreme Court for six years, during which time he authored a grand total of five decisions. Clarence Thomas can only aspire to that level of shiftlessness.

For all his hard work squeezing blood from turnips, it was not until he courted and married one Rachel Donelson that he became wealthy. Unfortunately, she was already married to a man named Captain Lewis Robards. That didn't stop her from eloping with Jackson. So for about three years, until her divorce was finalized, Andrew Jackson was a bigamist. She died just before he became president, leaving him a fortune worth about $130 million in today's money.

But perhaps the most revealing anecdote as to what a self-important asshole Jackson was came in 1796 when he was just a freshman in Congress. George Washington had given his "farewell speech" to be published in September 1796, and gave his final address before Congress in December that year. His farewell was for decades considered the most important speech in US history: not only was he walking away from power, he warned against the dangers of political fractiousness and the threat of foreign influence. This was the country's first president setting the standard for the peaceful transfer of power and warning of two problems that have plagued this country for nearly 250 years. Jackson refused to applaud.

His rise to the Presidency came at a time when most states were relaxing their voter eligibility to include all white male adults, even the ones who didn't own land or know how to read. That meant a huge influx of uneducated voters populating the electorate. Jackson courted them just as enthusiastically as Reagan would later do with evangelicals.

As president, he created what was known as the "spoils system" where he routinely fired people he viewed as disloyal and replaced them with cronies. No wonder Jackson is Trump's favorite president. Jackson's tax policy drove a wedge between

North and South and his handling of the economy precipitated the Great Panic of 1837, our country's first major economic meltdown. It is the latter, where he refused to recharter the central bank, allowing state banks to basically print money at will, that precipitated his later transgressions. Needless to say, inflation skyrocketed because state banks had no oversight and basically OKed every loan. In response, Jackson issued an executive order forcing the sale of any federal lands to be transacted only in gold or silver. Without being able to use state-backed paper money, the demand for gold and silver increased, which made the discovery of those metals on Native American lands in 1828 a focal point of contention.

His hatred of Native Americans had already led him on a crusade beginning in 1813 to not only kill as many as possible but to steal their land and sell it cheaply to the rich landowners in the South. That was how many of the vast plantations were created. Before Andrew Jackson, slavery was actually on the wane in the United States. He had been an enthusiastic supporter of the practice, owning 150 slaves himself. Once paying for an ad in the Tennessee Gazette for the return of an escaped slave, he offered an extra ten dollars incentive for every hundred lashes administered to them after capture. But when the 19th-century equivalent of factory farms came calling due to the availability of cheap new land, the demand for slave labor rose dramatically.

As President, Jackson forced tens of thousands of Native Americans from Georgia, Tennessee, and the Carolinas with the Indian Removal Act of 1830. The Cherokee People brought two cases before the Supreme Court to challenge it. Both times, in 1831 and 1832, the Court *ruled in their favor*, stating that Cherokees were a "domestic dependent nation" and as such could not be forced to give up their lands.

The Act had not been a sudden change of US policy. Beginning with George Washington, the native people of America had been systematically forced to give up their culture. Converting to Christianity, learning to read and speak English, adopting "settler values" like monogamous marriage, and abandoning non-marital sex (a pact that most of our Presidents to that point in time had been incapable of upholding) were all legislated. They had also been forced to adopt the concept of individual ownership of land and property (including in some instances, slaves).

And despite their forced acceptance of these cultural "values", Jackson sent the troops in to begin removing the people who had a legal right to own that land. Jackson defended his decision by defying the Court's ruling by famously stating, "[Chief Justice] John Marshall has made his decision. Now let him enforce it."

The first removal under the Act was actually an exchange of land with the Choctaw Nation in 1831, trading their remaining 11 million acres in Mississippi (several "treaties" with the US government had already reduced the size of their lands considerably) for 15 million acres in Oklahoma. It wasn't a bad deal considering what would be discovered in Oklahoma a few years later, but even then the Choctaw would never be allowed to enjoy its full potential. The Seminoles were removed in 1832, the Muscogee (also known as the Creek) in 1834, the Chickasaw in 1837, and finally the Cherokee in 1838. As you might expect with Jackson, however, the land they were "being given" was already occupied by the Quapaw (who had been removed from Ohio and Arkansas in 1834), and Osage (who had been removed from Missouri and Arkansas in 1825).

As an aside, the term "Indian giver" originally meant "a gift for which something of equal value is expected." The first recorded instances appeared in 1765. Some time between then and 1860, when it became defined as "one who gives a present then takes it back", something obviously changed. Tell me again where Andrew Jackson falls on that timeline?

More than 60,000 Cherokee, 17,000 Choctaw and 15,000 Creek lost everything they had but what they could carry and were forced to trudge more than a thousand miles. More than a quarter of them died en route. Actually, that's not the whole story. Many of them did die due to starvation, deprivation, and disease, but there were numerous incidents where local settlers along the way attacked and murdered them. So it wasn't just a passive death march. Many active causes have been whitewashed from this atrocity. Unfortunately, that was just the preamble of a national policy of ethnic cleansing that peaked during the Grant administration but continued through the end of the century.

Was that the worst part? Certainly, but the context makes it even worse because in forcing them from their lands, Jackson betrayed the trust of the same people who were responsible for his victories during the War of 1812 against a confederacy of Shawnee and Creek known as the Red Sticks. Without emerging victorious at the Battle of Horseshoe Bend, there would never have been a Hero of New Orleans. Going into that battle he had but a thousand of his Tennessee volunteers, which was less than half what he had when he had started his campaign. He was joined by more than three thousand Cherokee and Choctaw warriors with a few Creek volunteers who had opposed the Red Sticks. This victory, codified by the Treaty of Fort Jackson, netted him 23 million acres of land, which he promptly sold to plantation owners for a pittance. That was the beginning of Jackson's contribution to saving slavery.

The great irony of the Trail of Tears was that Jackson relocated the First Nation peoples to land that would later be discovered to be more valuable than the land they were forced from. In 1859, when Oklahoma was still only a territory, oil was discovered on the reservations. The territory was granted statehood in 1907 largely due to its massive reserves. Until 1930, Oklahoma, not Texas, was the biggest producer of oil in the United States, occasionally challenged for the top spot by California. Of course, the Native Americans were cheated and swindled (and occasionally murdered) out of their claims, just like they had been with nearly every single treaty they had signed with the US Government. But that's another story. Back to Jackson...

It's almost impossible to contemplate, but the damage he did extended far beyond our own borders and his own century. In addition to citing the Armenian genocide in Turkey in 1915, Adolf Hitler listed several precedents in American history that gave him the confidence to propose what would later be known as the 'Lebensraum' (literally "living space") and subsequently 'the Final Solution', what everyone now knows as the Holocaust. The latter came from early 20th-century eugenics laws in Virginia and California that had withstood legal challenges. But the former - the taking of land from people to give it to a preferred ethnic group - that inspiration came from Jackson's Indian Removal Act. Hitler specifically referred to Jackson, citing:

"It is inconceivable that a higher people should painfully exist on a soil too narrow for it, whilst amorphous masses, which contribute nothing to civilization, occupy infinite tracts of a soil that is one of the richest in the world."

Jackson's presidency opened the door for a string of incompetents, drunks, dullards, and never-do-wells to "lead" the country. John Tyler, Millard Filmore, Franklin Pierce, and James Buchanan are often cited among the 10 worst presidents in US history. Their bad policies and incompetence in the 1840s and 1850s led us toward the inevitable calamity of the Civil War but also to another kind of catastrophe with implications that were deleterious to the well-being of all US citizens, not just the ones directly affected by slavery: they did nothing to regulate the growing capitalist economy.

In 1856, the Crimean War, which had pitted England, France, and the Ottomans against Russia, came to an end. Before that conflict, Russia had provided much of the grain to Europe. However, during the three years of the war, the US Midwest had picked up the slack producing grains in support of the British allies. After the conflict ended, however, Russia resumed its role as the breadbasket for Europe. Without European customers, US grain sales and the US commodities market started to drop. With the other financial markets now apprehensive, the next domino fell in 1857, when the California Gold Rush, which had begun in 1849 (and had also taken place on forcibly-vacated Native American lands precipitating another ethnic cleansing), saw a precipitous decline in claims. That same year, the SS Central America, a passenger ship carrying 578 passengers and 30,000 pounds of gold went down during a hurricane. With another commodity's market going into shock, this one integral to the money supply, the teetering economy began to tip. It fell over the edge when the New York City branch of the Ohio Life Insurance and Trust Company suspended payments due to the criminal frauds perpetrated by its own executives. Speculators led a massive run on the banks. The railway industry (which had been seen as a safe haven for investment for decades) had increasingly been saddled with riskier loans intended to spur even faster growth, much like the mortgage industry had in 2007-08. When the run on the banks began, those loans were called to cover the shortfalls of cash. Had these events happened a decade earlier nothing more might have happened. Before the widespread use of the telegraph, news sometimes took weeks or months to arrive. But by 1857, it took only minutes for the bad news to travel and tip the dominoes of confusion and panic throughout the financial industry. The crash not only crippled the US economy but the world economy as well, not unlike the Great Depression would three-quarters of a century later. It would not be until years after the Civil War that the economy recovered.

    Abraham Lincoln understood the ramifications of unrestricted, unregulated commerce and corporate power. Between the banks, investors, and corporations, the US economy and the world economy had been devastated by the whims and urges of a few people who had no will or incentive to control their avarice or fear. He warned of the dangers in November of 1864, writing:

"We may congratulate ourselves that this cruel war is nearing its end. It has cost a vast amount of treasure and blood... It has indeed been a trying hour for the Republic; but I see in the near future a crisis approaching that unnerves me and causes me to tremble for the safety of my country... corporations have been enthroned and an era of corruption in high places will follow, and the money power of the country will endeavor to prolong its reign by working upon the prejudices of the people until all wealth is aggregated in a few hands and the Republic is destroyed. I feel at this moment more anxiety for the safety of my country than ever before, even in the midst of war. God grant that my suspicions may prove groundless."

Let's put that in the simplest terms: Lincoln was worried that corporations were a greater threat to democracy than the Confederacy. He thought CEOs and bankers posed a greater threat to the Great American Experiment than the people who had just fought an actual war for the right to own humans that had claimed the lives of more than half a million people. Why? Because he understood that slavery wasn't some flaw in Southern culture; it was a flaw in business culture. Since the dawn of man, rulers and leaders in societies have turned to slave labor to construct their empires because it was economically expedient. Lincoln knew that slavery was the inevitable goal of unrestricted capitalism because its structure was essentially no different than feudalism, just without the Divine Right nonsense. The evidence in the US from the subsequent century and a half points to that conclusion. There has been a deliberate drive to erode civil rights away from labor by those who wield the capital. We don't even need to look back that far.

During the COVID pandemic, we saw the largest increase in poverty in the history of the US occur at the same time as the largest increase in wealth for the top 1%. We also saw the largest recorded profits in 50 years for the Fortune 500. While watching more than a million Americans die, numerous corporations begged like street urchins for government handouts (many of which were forgiven), only to lay off tens of thousands of employees while transferring those government subsidies to shareholders in the form of stock buybacks. So millions died and tens of millions were impoverished during a worldwide pandemic while corporate execs and hedge fund managers got fat on government money and assurances.

After Lincoln's assassination and the end of the Civil War, the Reconstruction only served to crystallize Lincoln's concerns. Let's be clear: Reconstruction was working. Black leaders were elected to US Congress and at all levels of government. Laws were being changed to reflect a more egalitarian society. However, the pushback was fierce and often violent. According to an article in the Smithsonian Magazine, "The violence was so terrible, in fact, that it's possible that as many as 53,000 Blacks were killed in the South between the end of the Civil War and the end of Reconstruction - which averages out to about five per day… there are startling individual statistics, like the fact that the Texas Freedmen's Bureau recorded over a thousand murders of Blacks between 1865 and 1866, with reasons like "Black man didn't tip his hat so I shot him" given on *official* reports, as if somehow that was an acceptable reason.

The violence was systemic. Organizations like the Ku Klux Klan and the White League assassinated officials, tortured people, and burned houses, all in the name of restoring white supremacy, pushing Blacks back into an inferior position, and driving Lincoln's Republican Party from the South. The truly messed-up thing about this is that it worked.

Of course, they had help from President Andrew Johnson, who himself had been a slaveholder. After Lincoln was murdered he did everything he could to overturn or undermine the things Lincoln had accomplished. It's one of the reasons he was the first president to be impeached. Perhaps the most significant thing he did to undermine the Reconstruction was to reduce the number of men in the Union Army from nearly a million to 90,000 in less than a year, which severely hampered the federal government's ability to enforce their new laws in the South. By 1871 during Grant's first term, that number was down to 30,000 but most of those were deployed in the West. Less than 5,000 Union soldiers were stationed in the South. Even then, Southern leaders complained about a "Northern military occupation".

The Supreme Court was no better. The Court found the Civil Rights Act of 1875 unconstitutional, ruled that Congress lacked authority to grant equal protections under the law to Blacks, and ruled that the Enforcement Act of 1871 - which had intended to stop the KKK from organizing - was unconstitutional.

The Compromise of 1877 took it a step further: in exchange for letting Republican Rutherford B. Hayes become president, the Republicans would withdraw the remaining Union troops from the South, allowing white politicians to turn back the clock to pre-war atrocities against black communities. That was the kick to the gut that signaled the end of Reconstruction. The failure of the Lodge Bill in 1890 - which authorized the federal government to ensure that all elections were fair, and would have empowered federal courts to appoint supervisors – was the final nail in the coffin.

Driving the failure of Reconstruction were Northern Democrats (supported by the northern bankers who financed slavery) and Southern aristocrats seeking to undermine administrations looking to remake the economy and the country into something that would at least resemble the "all men are created equal" ideal. Over the course of twenty years, they proved that people who are motivated (and more importantly, *well-financed*), even when they are grossly outnumbered, their cause blatantly immoral (and in many cases illegal), can still affect society and our democracy in catastrophically harmful ways.

Not coincidentally, the decade that followed is often referred to as the "Gilded Age" of business. Taking their moral cues from the Southern plantation owners, robber barons accumulated vast wealth exploiting industrialization, technological advancement, political favors, the lack of restrictions on corporations, and an influx of very cheap foreign labor. According to various measurements, in 1890 the wealthiest 1% of Americans owned one-fourth of the nation's assets; the top 10% owned over 70 percent. By 1900, the richest 10% had increased their holdings to 90% of the nation's wealth. Ironically, it was Lincoln's Republicans who did the most to facilitate this, handing out federal, state, and local subsidies and bonds for railroads and government-backed protections for shareholders.

How does this apply to Reagan? Because like Jackson, he didn't care what the law said. Rules were for other people and if they didn't like it, he'd dare them to do something about it. They did, with the Iran-Contra hearings, although neither Reagan nor his Vice President George H. W. Bush experienced much political fallout despite being in the rooms where the plots were laid out. And like some of the Founding Fathers who sought control over the uninformed masses, and many in the post-Civil Rights Act Republican Party, he saw the democratization of power as an abomination. America was at its best when only 2% of the populace controlled things, and preferably if they were white.

It didn't end there. The 13th Amendment abolished slavery but it granted one very important exception:

"Neither slavery nor involuntary servitude, except as a punishment for crime whereof the party shall have been duly convicted, shall exist within the United States, or any place subject to their jurisdiction."

That means if you are convicted of a felony, you can be put to work for no pay by the prison system, which has been a loophole widely abused from the beginning of the Jim Crow era. It is a cycle that continues to this day and is a driving force behind many racially-motivated anti-drug laws. It relates to Reagan because he campaigned as being tough on crime. As an aside, the violent crime wave he was supposedly combating that arose in the 1960s and 1970s has been largely attributed to the presence of lead in gasoline. Researchers as early as the 1950s proved it was dangerous to human health and determined that it caused a 10-15 point decrease in IQ worldwide, and was a significant driver of violent behavior. The EPA began phasing it out in 1973 but it wasn't fully outlawed until 1996.

Anyway, in 1983, three right-wing Reaganites - Thomas Beasley, Robert Crants, and Don Hutto - formed the Corrections Corporation of America, a for-profit prisons company. Like many neoliberal ideas, this one was both a failure in concept and execution but very much a success in strictly business terms. The latter was what mattered most for the conservatives willing to dump billions of dollars into supporting it.

Why is neoliberal management of public services always a failure? Because government is supposed to serve the people, the end-users. Privatization changes the objective: the people are merely the means to the end (in this case: profit). Only the shareholders are truly served. Whether the people get served or not is largely irrelevant. A state- or federally-run prison system's goal is to rehabilitate the inmate and return him/her to normal life, at least as best as can be managed. Conversely, the primary mission of a privately-run system, like any company, is to have as many prisoners as possible to maximize revenue. For the prison to make a profit there have to be more criminals. So to make that happen, longer and more severe sentences were mandated, mostly by conservative politicians. Poorer populations tend to be targeted by law enforcement to fill the prisons because they have fewer resources available to mount a capable legal defense. Far more often than is acceptable we also see judges get bribed to send people to jail for petty offenses, which puts the victims of this judicial abuse in an ever-spiraling cycle of always being labeled a criminal. The more felons a prison has, the more slave labor they have. Reagan was the reason this massive miscarriage of justice gained a market. Bill Clinton certainly abetted it with the 1994 Violent Crime Control and Law Enforcement Act he signed to appeal to conservative voters but it all started with Reagan. In

1980, total spending on corrections in the US was $17 billion. Today it's $81 billion, a rate of increase twice as large as the US spends on education. According to the Department of Justice, the number of people under federal Correctional Authority (meaning people on parole and those in prison) was 5,444,900 in 2021, of which 1.7 million were incarcerated. The total number of slaves in 1860 was 3,953,760. Welcome to the new slavery. Today, prison labor contributes $11 billion worth of goods and services, and produces everything from ballistic armor for police to office furniture. More than 4,100 companies benefit from prison labor including Verizon, IBM, Walmart, and McDonalds. Additionally, it is estimated that those previously incarcerated lose another $372.3 billion per year in income due to the fact that employers pay up to 50% less for their labor after they've "paid their debt to society". If that weren't enough, we have seen confirmed stories of inmates having their organs harvested without consent. We've come full circle from Washington's teeth. History doesn't usually repeat itself but it often rhymes with something that happened before.

Andrew Jackson: Lawyer, Judge and Legislator
https://www.historynet.com/andrew-jackson-lawyer-judge-and-legislator/

Ten Things to Know about Andrew Jackson
https://www.thoughtco.com/things-to-know-about-andrew-jackson-104318

Andrew Jackson: the Good, the Bad and the Ugly
https://www.abbevilleinstitute.org/andrew-jackson-the-good-the-bad-and-the-ugly/

Hunting down runaway slaves: The cruel ads of Andrew Jackson and 'the master class'
https://www.washingtonpost.com/news/retropolis/wp/2017/04/11/hunting-down-runaway-slaves-the-cruel-ads-of-andrew-jackson-and-the-master-class/

Treaty of Fort Jackson
https://encyclopediaofalabama.org/article/treaty-of-fort-jackson/

The Trail of Tears
https://theamericanhistory.org/what-was-the-trail-of-tears.html

Reaction to George Washington's final speech before Congress
https://www.washingtonpost.com/history/2020/02/17/george-washington-unpopular-president/

Ulysses S. Grant Launched an Illegal War Against the Plains Indians, Then Lied About It
https://www.smithsonianmag.com/history/ulysses-grant-launched-illegal-war-plains-indians-180960787/

How Hitler Took Inspiration From Native American Extermination To Forge His Final Solution
https://allthatsinteresting.com/hitler-native-american-extermination

What Lincoln Foresaw: Corporations Being "Enthroned" After the Civil War and Re-Writing the Laws Defining Their Existence
https://ratical.org/corporations/Lincoln.html

Wilmington 1898: When white supremacists overthrew a US government
https://www.bbc.com/news/world-us-canada-55648011

The Messed Up Truth About The Reconstruction Era
https://www.grunge.com/225063/the-messed-up-truth-about-the-reconstruction-era/

Reconstruction Didn't Fail. It Was Overthrown
https://time.com/5256940/reconstruction-failure-excerpt/

Industrial Growth and Big Business During the Gilded Age
https://courses.lumenlearning.com/wm-ushistory2/chapter/industrial-growth-and-big-business/#footnote-1520-2

Did removing lead from petrol spark a decline in crime?
https://www.bbc.com/news/magazine-27067615

A Brief History of America's Private Prison Industry
https://www.motherjones.com/politics/2016/06/history-of-americas-private-prison-industry-timeline/

The Corruption Within Private Prisons
https://www.catalystproject.net/blogus/the-corruption-within-private-prisons

Privatized prisons lead to more inmates, longer sentences, study finds
https://news.cahnrs.wsu.edu/article/privatized-prisons-lead-to-more-inmates-longer-sentences-study-finds/

Pa. Judge Sentenced To 28 Years In Massive Juvenile Justice Bribery Scandal
https://www.npr.org/sections/thetwo-way/2011/08/11/139536686/pa-judge-sentenced-to-28-years-in-massive-juvenile-justice-bribery-scandal

Judges behind "kids-for-cash" scandal ordered to pay more than $200M
https://www.axios.com/2022/08/17/judges-kids-for-cash-scandal

This Youth Detention Center Superintendent Illegally Locks Kids Alone in Cells
https://www.propublica.org/article/knoxville-detention-center-illegally-locks-kids-alone-in-cells

Prisoners in 2021 – Statistical Tables
https://bjs.ojp.gov/library/publications/prisoners-2021-statistical-tables

Correctional Populations in the United States, 2021 – Statistical Tables
https://bjs.ojp.gov/document/cpus21st.pdf

Incarceration stats by race, ethnicity, and gender for all 50 states and D.C.
https://www.prisonpolicy.org/blog/2023/09/27/updated_race_data/

Private Companies Producing with US Prison Labor in 2020: Prison Labor in the US
https://corpaccountabilitylab.org/calblog/2020/8/5/private-companies-producing-with-us-prison-labor-in-2020-prison-labor-in-the-us-part-ii

US prison workers produce $11bn worth of goods and services a year for pittance
https://www.theguardian.com/us-news/2022/jun/15/us-prison-workers-low-wages-exploited

Some of the Most Recognizable Brands Rely on Prison Labor to Make Money
https://marketrealist.com/p/companies-that-use-prison-labor/

Prisoners in the US are part of a hidden workforce linked to hundreds of popular food brands
https://apnews.com/article/prison-to-plate-inmate-labor-investigation-c6f0eb4747963283316e494eadf08c4e

Alabama prisoners' bodies returned to families with hearts, other organs missing, lawsuit claims
https://www.cbsnews.com/news/prisoners-bodies-returned-to-families-missing-organs-lawsuit-alleges/

215 people have been buried behind a Mississippi jail since 2016
https://www.npr.org/2024/01/12/1224449631/mississippi-jail-graves-investigation

The Ethics of Organ Donation from Condemned Prisoners
https://optn.transplant.hrsa.gov/professionals/by-topic/ethical-considerations/the-ethics-of-organ-donation-from-condemned-prisoners/

US Prison Policies on Organ Donation for Individuals Who Are Incarcerated
https://jamanetwork.com/journals/jamanetworkopen/fullarticle/2802129

New data on formerly incarcerated people's employment reveal labor market injustices
https://www.prisonpolicy.org/blog/2022/02/08/employment/

How Involvement with the Criminal Justice System Deepens Inequality
https://www.brennancenter.org/our-work/research-reports/conviction-imprisonment-and-lost-earnings-how-involvement-criminal

LOST EARNINGS BY THE NUMBERS
https://www.brennancenter.org/sites/default/files/2020-09/01_Lost%20Wages%20Fact%20Sheet.pdf

The 2nd "Founding Fathers"

At the end of the 19th century, the power of corporations reached its first zenith. In 1904, John D. Rockefeller's Standard Oil controlled 91% of the US oil refining business and 85% of its sales. From 1882 to 1906, it doled out $548,436,000 (roughly $18 billion converted to 2023 dollars) in dividends to its investors, roughly 65% of its earnings. Congress reacted to Standard's unbridled wealth and power by passing the Sherman Antitrust Act in 1890. However, it wasn't until Teddy Roosevelt came to office in 1901 that it was finally enforced. He created the Department of Commerce and Labor (later divided into two separate agencies) in 1903 in large part for this very purpose. As proof that regulation does not stifle industry, of the thirty-two major oil and gas companies that are based in the United States, Exxon Mobil (a descendant of Standard Oil) is by far the largest. It is also the world's largest publicly traded oil company and the largest refiner. It controls just 22% of the US market and a little more than 6% of the world market. Just last year alone, its most profitable ever, investors received $14.8 billion in dividends on less than 4% of its earnings.

In 1901, Roosevelt addressed the nation on the threat Standard and its ilk posed:

"The great corporations which we have grown to speak of rather loosely as trusts are the creatures of the State, and the State not only has the right to control them wherever need of such control is shown. The immediate necessity in dealing with trusts is to place them under the real, not the nominal, control of some sovereign to which, as its creatures, the trusts owe allegiance, and in whose courts the sovereign's orders may be enforced. In my opinion, this sovereign must be the National Government."

But even Roosevelt wasn't above the lure of corporate money. During the presidential campaign of 1904, his Democratic opponent Alton Parker charged that Roosevelt had been granting favors to big business in exchange for campaign donations. He denied the allegations, of course, but then demanded that his Secretary of Commerce and Labor return the equivalent of $3.3 million in campaign donations from Standard Oil. After the election, it was revealed that another $4.9 million in Standard Oil campaign contributions found its way into Republican coffers to green-light a pipeline through Osage lands in Oklahoma, something that could only be done at the federal level and that Roosevelt himself had allegedly overruled his Secretary of the Interior to approve.

But by 1908, he had enough. In a special message to Congress, he stated:

"Predatory wealth--of the wealth accumulated on a giant scale by all forms of iniquity, ranging from the oppression of wage workers to unfair and unwholesome methods of crushing out competition, and to defrauding the public by stock-jobbing and the manipulation of securities. Certain wealthy men of this stamp, whose conduct should be abhorrent to every man of ordinarily decent conscience, and who commit the hideous wrong of teaching our young men that phenomenal business success must ordinarily be based on dishonesty, have during the last few months made it apparent that they have banded together to work for a reaction. Their endeavor is to overthrow and discredit all who honestly administer the law, to prevent any additional legislation which would check and restrain them, and to secure if possible a freedom from all restraint which will permit every unscrupulous wrongdoer to do what he wishes unchecked provided he has enough money....The methods by which the Standard Oil people and those engaged in the other combinations of which I have spoken above have achieved great fortunes can only be justified by the advocacy of a system of morality which would also justify every form of criminality on the part of a labor union, and every form of violence, corruption, and fraud, from murder to bribery and ballot box stuffing in politics."

The problem was that Presidents eventually leave office; corporations never do. They simply accumulate more wealth and influence until they, not the voters, determine our national policies: which foreign governments to support and what policies to enact.

So it's no surprise that the subsequent Republican presidents - Harding, Coolidge, and Hoover – bent over backward to assist the interests of corporations.

Warren Harding was arguably the most corrupt president ever before Richard Nixon came along. Not only did he have one of the biggest political scandals in history with Teapot Dome (in which the President leased oil from what was then the equivalent of the Strategic Oil Reserves to a couple of private companies for a very low rate without any competitive bidding in exchange for bribes), but also was at the center of scandals involving the Justice Department and the handling of veterans affairs. On a personal level, he was known to have had at least two mistresses, fathering a child with one while in the White House. He fought to eliminate corporate taxes, fought against giving the soldiers who fought in World War 1 any bonuses for their service, and passed the first of several subsequent restrictive Republican immigration laws.

Calvin Coolidge's primary contribution to American culture was its most damaging slogan – "the business of America is business". Actually, the theory behind the United States for several of the Founding Fathers was to build the country's wealth to a point where it would become a haven/garden for the world's greatest artists. That did become true with some of the greatest writers and composers of the 19th and 20th centuries but what was also true was that building wealth was never the second priority.

To that end, Coolidge cut taxes dramatically, believing – and you're gonna love this – that if you cut taxes on the wealthy, the government will get more revenue. By 1929, the tax rate was 24% on people earning more than $100,000. That's all was well and good for the well-to-do going crazy during the Roaring 20s but not so great when it all came crashing down with the Great Depression. It's not like this couldn't have been predicted. Every 15-20 years since the early 1800s, the US economy crashed after a boom period. This one merely had a higher peak and a lower bottom due to Coolidge's laissez-faire approach.

His hands-off policy was also not so good for the farmers who were struggling to make ends meet due to severe droughts. Under his instruction, the federal government refused to help them with any kind of subsidies. It only got worse during the Great Mississippi Flood of 1927. More than 500 people died and more than more than 600,000 Americans were left homeless or devastated with 27,000 square miles of land inundated in depths up to thirty feet. The damages from that disaster ran close to a billion dollars in today's currency. It was the worst natural disaster in American history until Hurricane Katrina in 2005. He put his Secretary of Commerce in charge of the clean-up operation, who did such a good job that it catapulted him to succeed Coolidge as our next President: Herbert Hoover

He was a compassionate man, not unlike Jimmy Carter. He oversaw programs to feed Europe after World War 1, helped Americans recover after the Great Flood of 1927, and was also instrumental in the growth and regulation of the radio and airline industries. But when it came to race relations he felt minorities didn't need help and that they should affirm their equality by pulling themselves up by their bootstraps. That would become a familiar refrain among Republicans of the latter parts of the 20th century. It didn't stop there. He blamed the Great Depression on Mexicans and forced the repatriation of a million in a forced migration (not unlike Andrew Jackson a century before). He believed that big business should continue unimpeded by regulations or taxes and that the Depression could be solved by voluntary private donations from the wealthy (I'll give you a few moments to stop laughing). Yes, even back then Republicans believed in trickle-down economics, and even then, everyone else knew it was a scam. Famed humorist Will Rogers said during the early years of the Great Depression, "The money was all appropriated for the top in the hopes that it would trickle down to the needy. Mr. Hoover didn't know that money trickled up. Give it to the people at the bottom and the people at the top will have it before night, anyhow. But it will at least have passed through the poor fellow's hands." Hoover made the additional critical mistake of refusing to provide federal relief which only made the effects of the Crash worse. He then compounded the problem by increasing taxes to address the budget deficit after years of a budget surplus. The cherry on top of his Depression sundae was increasing tariffs, which caused a predictable downturn in international trade. Worse still was his unwillingness to take aggressive action to stabilize the banking industry, both domestically and internationally, which provided fertile ground for the rise of Adolf Hitler in Germany's debt-wracked economy. As effective as he was as an administrator for humanitarian causes, he was a complete disaster as a leader of the free world.

Another Republican wouldn't win office until Eisenhower in 1952. His running mate and vice president was Richard Nixon. The two were as opposite as two members of the same political party could be. Eisenhower was a pragmatist and content to pretty much let things go as they will. Nixon was an ideologue who gained fame as Joseph McCarthy's wingman in his hunt for communists.

Eisenhower hated McCarthy and his demagoguery. He was personally offended by McCarthy's attack on his friend and mentor, George Marshall, whose eponymous plan had successfully rebuilt war-ravaged Europe and had managed to stave off communism in many of those countries. It was a hugely popular ideology among the average European because it promised a share of the bounty in the recovery and rebuilding of their countries. To combat that appeal, Marshall convinced many governments to reject it in exchange for US financial support and trade. To call Marshall a communist was not only an outrage but utterly ludicrous. That didn't stop McCarthy, who saw every obstacle as a nail for his anti-communist hammer to pound. In his view, Marshall was a socialist steeped in falsehoods. That left Eisenhower with a choice: to defend his friend and sound like a sympathizer, or remain silent so that he could court anti-communist voters. He chose the latter. And to prove he wasn't a communist sympathizer, he stepped up authorizing the FBI and other agencies to investigate suspected communists, thus giving more inertia to the Red Scare. Eisenhower made the additional mistake of refusing to denounce McCarthy, saying it would only give him more attention. By 1953, nearly half of Americans polled had a favorable impression of McCarthy. If any of that sounds familiar – a President and the media refusing to denounce a famous political figure's outrageous claims - let me know. It was only when McCarthy went after the Army looking for communists that Ike exercised executive privilege citing national security concerns, then counterattacked by pressuring the Senate to censure him. Eventually, McCarthy was exposed as a huckster and a fabulist, quickly losing influence. But the damage had been done.

That might not have been Ike's biggest mistake. Appointing two very influential anti-communist brothers to positions of foreign influence was: Allen Dulles as head of the CIA and John Foster Dulles as his Secretary of State. Beginning under Truman when Allen was a senior member of the CIA precursor (the OSS) and John was a senior partner with the NY-based law firm Sullivan and Cromwell, they had established shell companies to hide the funding for right-wing insurgents, in addition to their regular duties representing giant companies like the Anglo-Iranian Oil Company and United Fruit, a company that dominated food production in Latin America and the Caribbean. They had also represented IG Farben, the German conglomerate that produced the Xyclon-B gas used in the Nazi death camps. The brothers' schemes, while securing dependent allies in the near term, ultimately proved disastrous by the end of the 20th century. Many of the countries they tampered with ended up either hating the US as a mortal enemy or openly distrusting US motives. The list of actual coups they were responsible for predicted several hot spots in late 20th-century geopolitics:

The assassination of Patrice Lumumba in the Congo (later changed to Zaire) in 1951,

The overthrow of Mohammad Mossadegh in Iran in 1953,

The overthrow of Jacobo Arbenz in Guatemala in 1954.

Portrayed as communists (even though they were just nationalists trying to combat poverty in their countries), these leaders were replaced by militaristic dictators. Allen was also one of the architects of what would be later known as the 1961 Bay of Pigs invasion, a failed coup to overthrow Fidel Castro in Cuba. In addition, his acolytes would be responsible for the later overthrows of Joao Goulart in Brazil in 1964, Sukarno in Indonesia in 1967, and Salvatore Allende in Chile in 1973.

While supportive of US policies internationally, these new regimes brutally oppressed their citizens domestically which became problematic for US presidents claiming to stand for "democracy and freedom" in countries around the world. But don't for a second think that Allen Dulles was some unstoppable master of espionage operations or some genius puppet master. During his two decades in intelligence, in addition to his failure in Cuba (over which he was fired by Kennedy), the agencies he ran fumbled coup operations in Romania, China, Vietnam, Laos, Burma, Indonesia, Tibet, Egypt, Syria, and Iraq. Still, he was influential in conservative and anti-communist politics until he died in 1969. Ike had given him that leverage, and it was acolytes like Henry Kissinger who carried on his mission under Nixon and Ford. The Sullivan and Cromwell connection continues to influence right-wing politics to this day with former employees like Peter Thiel and several members of the BlackRock board.

After Kennedy was assassinated in 1963, Dulles was one of the seven people appointed to the Warren Commission. Why Johnson appointed him specifically (his was the first name Johnson offered in a conversation with FBI Director J Edgar Hoover when they were formulating the Warren Commission) is anybody's guess but suffice it to say that if he wanted to uncover the truth, Dulles was the exact opposite of "the man for the job". When the Commission issued its report in 1964, only 56% of the public believed its findings, dropping down to 36% by 1966. The inordinate number of irregularities, inaccuracies, and gaps in the narrative it proposed were so illogical that three of the seven members of the Commission disavowed its findings. Dulles was the primary reason.

In 1975, twelve years after the assassination, the Zapruder film was shown for the first time to the American public on, of all places, Geraldo Rivera's "Good Night America" show. The public was both shocked and outraged, enough so that the following year Congress held the US House Select Committee on Assassinations. Despite one of the lead witnesses being a former CIA handler whose answers were almost always misleading, the committee found enough evidence to declare that it was probable that more than just Oswald was involved - the opposite conclusion of the Warren Report - and that it had been guilty of numerous instances of insufficient consideration given to witness testimony and/or to possible witnesses.

I won't go into my theories about the assassination, but I will say that despite numerous successful lawsuits under the Freedom of Information Act to get the more than five million pages of documents and testimony related to the investigation released to the public, that there are still more than 4500 files that remain secret. If you watch any detective show on TV, you know it's often unwise to come to any definitive conclusions before the last 5-10 minutes because there's always a surprise reveal. I suspect this won't be any different.

Noted Republican operative Roger Stone wrote in one of his books that Richard Nixon once told him that Lyndon Johnson was responsible. Johnson certainly benefited, but the quote went on to say that both Nixon and Johnson hated Kennedy and wanted to be President; only Johnson was willing to kill for it. Of course, one has to consider the source: a well-documented liar reporting a story told by another well-documented liar about a President who had some sketchy friends and who also happened to be the Republican's favorite punching bag since the 1960s.

As for Nixon, he was certainly cut from the same virulently anti-communist cloth as Dulles. He had been a key figure in the Red Scare witch hunts (HUAC) for communists in the US government. He had "successfully" prosecuted Alger Hiss, one of the architects of the formation of the United Nations and a huge believer in FDR's New Deal. Nixon's victory in 1968 was primarily due to the public perception that he would finally get the US out of a war with the communists in Vietnam. What the public didn't know was that had secretly negotiated with the North Vietnamese to delay making a deal with LBJ on the promise that he would give them a better deal. Reagan employed a similar tactic with the hostage takers in Iran regarding the release of the American consulate taken during that country's 1979 revolution.

After he was elected, Nixon's better deal ended up being the increased bombing of not only North Vietnam but also Cambodia and Laos. Initially, Henry Kissinger, who at the time was a National Security Advisor, cautioned against this, but once Nixon began the bombing, he found ways to support its expansion. Eventually, Nixon placed him in charge of the State Department, a decision that would provide foreign policy disasters for three presidents. He bungled nearly every aspect of the Vietnam War, a war that could have ended in 1969 but persisted until 1975, costing tens of thousands of American lives.

The *only* substantial difference between what was offered when Nixon first won office and the final agreement was that North Vietnam had demanded that the US actively overthrow the South Vietnamese government and help them install a communist one in the original. In addition, Kissinger directed arms sales in support of the West Pakistani government committing genocide against Bengalis fighting for an independent Bangladeshi state. He supported the military coup d'etats of murderous dictator Augusto Pinochet in Chile, and Pol Pot in Cambodia. He also supported the military coup in Argentina in 1976 and fomented the 1975 civil war in Angola, the southern neighbor of Zaire. Finally, he was at least partially responsible for the 1979-1980 hostage crisis when he convinced President Jimmy Carter to allow "our good ally, the Shah of Iran" to seek medical treatment in the United States after he had fled his country. That decision further enraged the student demonstrators in Iran who were already incensed not only by the regime's atrocities but by the Shah's theft of nearly a billion dollars from the country's treasury. Two weeks later, they stormed the US Embassy in Tehran and took fifty-two hostages.

Nixon is often credited with beginning the "war on drugs" with his creation of the DEA, but the fight against drug use had actually begun with the Harrison Act in 1914 which outlawed opium and cocaine. Not coincidentally, both the Harrison Act and Nixon's war had racist elements. The opium targeted in Harrison had a primarily Chinese user population and cocaine was popular among African Americans of that era. John Ehrlichman, one of Nixon's inner circle revealed in an interview in Harper's Magazine that when Nixon began his campaign against heroin and marijuana, he was targeting two groups specifically:

"The Nixon campaign in 1968, and the Nixon White House after that, had two enemies: the antiwar left and black people. You understand what I'm saying? We knew we couldn't make it illegal to be either against the war or black, but by getting the public to associate the hippies with marijuana and blacks with heroin, and then criminalizing both heavily, we could disrupt those communities. We could arrest their leaders, raid their homes, break up their meetings, and vilify them night after night on the evening news. Did we know we were lying about the drugs? Of course, we did."

What Nixon had to know, however, was that his own CIA was responsible for much of the heroin being shipped into the country. That operation dated back to the days of the OSS just after World War 2. The OSS had been fairly incompetent in its role in intelligence gathering partly because the people running it (like Allen Dulles) hated communism more than they hated fascism and wanted a way forward to combat the USSR after the war. So they did whatever they could to protect Nazis in positions of power who didn't have too high a profile to attract protest but were also sympathetic to US interests... people like General Karl Wolff (SS leader Heinrich Himmler's Chief of Staff). But honestly, I'm pretty sure they would have been sympathetic to being injected with syphilis if it meant avoiding the noose. Truman rightly distrusted Dulles and the other leaders of the OSS for a variety of reasons, which was why he was reluctant to give the CIA a large budget from the outset. Rather than depend on government funding, which also had considerable oversight attached to it, Dulles and others green-lighted and expanded what Chiang Kai-shek had initiated in order to fund his nationalist war against Chinese communist leader Mao Zedong: the cultivation and sale of opium. The early CIA facilitated the heroin trade in Southeast Asia and Afghanistan and transported the drugs through what would eventually be called the French Connection in Marseilles. While this sounds a bit far-fetched already, it gets even more when you consider that in 1942 the Department of the Navy made a deal with the New York mafia in exchange for assuring port security at the major US harbors. They also provided on-the-ground intelligence in Italy during World War Two. In exchange, the US Government would secretly re-introduce them into Sicily and Southern Italy. If you've ever wondered why the mafia has such a high-profile presence in cities like New York, Chicago, New Orleans, and Los Angeles, now you know: it started with port security. After the war, the mafia remained and re-established themselves in Italy after being nearly wiped out by Mussolini's judicial and criminal reforms. They were only too happy to help out with a new revenue stream, helping to establish the drug trade from Sicily and France to New York and Los Angeles. Nixon used it to increase government spending with the creation of the DEA, all with public approval.

Reagan took all the tools that Nixon provided regarding the drug trade and green-lighted the CIA expansion of that "war" to Central America, adding cocaine to the menu of revenue streams. In addition to trading military weapons for hostages held in Iran and Lebanon, he allowed the CIA to illegally sell them weapons from 1981-1986, undermining the US's own trade embargo against that country. They used that money as well as the money from the cocaine trade to fund the anti-communist Contras in Nicaragua. The operation was detailed in Gary Webb's book Dark Alliance. Sadly, after eight years of attacks on his journalistic integrity following its publication, Webb took his own life by shooting himself in the head twice with a .38 revolver. Yep, twice.

But for all of Reagan's flag-waving about the "just cause" of removing the communist Sandanistas by force, the people of Nicaragua simply voted them out of office in 1990. The Tower Commission, which was engaged to look into the matter, also discovered that Reagan had green-lighted the sale of nerve gas, mustard gas, and chemical weapons to Iraq, a fact that would be relevant in George Bush's invasion of Iraq in 2003.

But back to Nixon, I'm not going to spend much time on Watergate, even though that is by far his most notable legacy. Obviously, corruption from the White House was nothing new. The administration of Ulysses Grant is considered by many historians as one of the most corrupt. However, in his case, he was the one who had called it out. It was his family and friends who were the ones who had crossed the line and he was the one who instigated the investigations. Warren Harding's was another extremely corrupt administration, but he was simply a willing participant. With Nixon, however, he was the ring leader of the criminal conspiracy. He didn't plan their capers, but he had knowledge of them, personally approved them, and led the effort to cover up the wrongdoing. He was the first US President, to use a mafia term, to be the Capo di Tutti Capo (boss of bosses) of the conspiracy. Had he not resigned, he likely would have been impeached, convicted, and then removed from office to be criminally indicted. It's also likely he would have subsequently met the same fate as his Watergate conspirators: convicted and jailed. Gerald Ford's pardon spared him the humiliation but it cost Ford the next election.

Writer Richard Stengel summed it up well: "Watergate was a simpler time. Gerald Ford's concern that prosecuting Nixon would 'tear the country apart' was due in part to the fact that Americans still venerated the presidency and elected leaders in general. Perhaps that was naive. The fact that Nixon was not prosecuted ushered in an era of belief in the imperial presidency that was not at all what our founders envisioned. It also paved the way for the concerns today that prosecuting a former president who has committed a multitude of crimes small and large will 'tear the country apart.' It was probably a mistake not to prosecute Nixon and it was in many ways the easier course not to. But if we truly believe no man is above the law we must demonstrate it."

A young TV producer named Roger Ailes took Nixon's escape from justice to heart. After debating with Nixon in 1967 about the future of TV – Nixon insisted it was a fad – Ailes convinced him that the future of politics was TV and its power to shape public opinion. It had certainly cost Nixon the presidency in 1960 during his famous televised debate with Kennedy. So Nixon hired him to be his TV producer in 1967, and the rest, as they often say, is history. The lesson Ailes learned that he brought with him to Reagan's 1984 re-election campaign was that with a network devoted to conservative politics, the GOP could have re-shaped public opinion during Watergate, either through counter-messaging or simply filling up the airwaves with other "more dire" concerns. It is not a coincidence that Reagan's FCC chairman Mark Fowler ruled in 1985 that the Fairness Doctrine hurt public interest and violated free speech. In fact, it had done the opposite, mandating that any time a political opinion was offered in a broadcast equal time must be devoted to the contrary opinion. Nevertheless, by 1987, the doctrine was officially abolished and in 1996, Fox News was born: a network devoted to the conservative viewpoint run by none other than Roger Ailes.

The problem with abolishing the Fairness Act was that it allowed for the creation of a propaganda machine. It wasn't a political (free speech) problem as much as it was a math problem. If one network is flooding its airwaves with bias and propaganda while the others are trying to present a balanced view, then math dictates that the public will eventually begin to lean in the direction of the propaganda. For example, assume there are three balanced networks (presenting 50/50 arguments on every issue) and at least try to get the news factually correct. And for the sake of argument, let's assume that 90% of all viewers believe the Earth is round, which means 10% believe it isn't. Now let's introduce a network that is devoted to propaganda, and in addition to reporting factual events often enough to be considered a news network, they frequently broadcast that the Earth is not round but shaped like a puppy. Who doesn't love a cuddly puppy? That's a much better notion than the Earth being as flat as a coin. So now only 75% of the available broadcasts confirm the fact that the Earth is round because now 25% of them are coming from the puppy propaganda station. The population of puppy-believers now have a platform they can reference, claiming, "See, these people say the Earth really is shaped like a puppy, just like I have for years". For those who either don't care to look into it, or trust their family or their friends who might be watching that channel, they might think "Wow, I didn't expect that you might say something useful but yeah, they do make a compelling argument because I also heard it on the news." Even if the percentages aren't high, there will be some that are convinced to at least listen to the propaganda more. So now we go from 10% puppy-people to maybe 12-15% puppy people. Now imagine that the argument is something much less fantastic, like that immigrants are taking your jobs, or that people on Social Security or welfare are bankrupting the country...

The ability to manipulate public opinion had evolved. Where Nixon was raked over the coals for his complicity in illegal actions, Reagan had been able to either disavow or conveniently forget all the things that happened on his watch through careful media manipulation with advisors like Roger Ailes. Where Ford had pardoned Nixon, George H. W. Bush pardoned all of Reagan's Iran Contra conspirators. That door was opened wider by the Fox Network to help George W. Bush craft his tax cuts that precipitated the 2007-2008 financial meltdown, diminish the public's awareness of his complete incompetence in the "War on Terror" as well as his unwarranted invasion of Iraq in his desperate search for chemical weapons. It also paved the way for Donald Trump to set the house on fire with his criminality before, during, and after his presidency, putting the country in a constitutional crisis that we face today. With his abolition of the Fairness Doctrine, Reagan provided Bush and Trump the accelerant to burn it all down.

The Multiple Scandals of President Warren G. Harding
https://www.history.com/news/warren-harding-scandals

Historical U.S. Federal Individual Income Tax Rates & Brackets, 1862-2021
https://taxfoundation.org/data/all/federal/historical-income-tax-rates-brackets/

Before FDR, Herbert Hoover Tried His Own 'New Deal'
https://www.history.com/news/great-depression-herbert-hoover-new-deal

Pivotal Role of Allen Dulles in Shielding Nazi War criminals
https://ahrp.org/pivotal-role-of-allen-dulles-in-shielding-nazi-war-criminals/

Chiang Kai-shek and the Drug Warlords of the Golden Triangle
https://www.chiangraitimes.com/tourism/chiang-kai-shek-and-the-drug-warlords-of-the-golden-triangle/

The Devil's Chessboard: Allen Dulles, the CIA, and the rise of America's secret government
by David Talbot
https://archive.org/details/devilschessboard0000talb

Operation Gladio: The Unholy Alliance Between the Vatican, the CIA, and the Mafia by Paul L. Williams
https://archive.org/details/OperationGladioTheUnholyAllianceBetweenTheVaticanTheCIAAndTheMafia

The Yankee And Cowboy War by Carl Oglesby
https://archive.org/details/OglesbyCarlTheYankeeAndCowboyWar

All in the Family: the Dulleses, the Bundys and the End of the Establishment
https://www.foreignaffairs.com/reviews/review-essay/2014-06-16/all-family
https://wcfia.harvard.edu/publications/all-family-dulleses-bundys-and-end-establishment

Dark alliance : the CIA, the Contras, and the crack cocaine explosion by Gary Webb
https://archive.org/details/darkallianceciac0000webb

The Tower Commission Report
https://archive.org/details/towercommission00unit

The Real Reason We Started the War on Drugs
https://archive.attn.com/stories/1503/war-on-drugs-real-reason

Aide says Nixon's war on drugs targeted blacks, hippies
https://www.aei.org/carpe-diem/the-shocking-and-sickening-story-behind-nixons-war-on-drugs-that-targeted-blacks-and-anti-war-activists/

New Documents Shed Light on CIA's Connection to Lee Harvey Oswald
https://www.newsweek.com/new-documents-shed-light-cias-connection-lee-harvey-oswald-1765105

JFK – Material Witness Deaths
https://docs.google.com/spreadsheets/d/
1FmXudDf6pqisxq_mepIC6iuG47RkDskPDWzQ9L7Lykw/edit#gid=1

JFK Witness Deaths and the London Times Actuary
https://www.lewrockwell.com/2013/04/richard-charnin/the-mysterious-deaths-of-jfk-murder-witnesses/

Scandals of the Ulysses S. Grant administration
https://en.wikipedia.org/wiki/Scandals_of_the_Ulysses_S._Grant_administration

Yes, Nixon Scuttled the Vietnam Peace Talks
https://www.politico.com/magazine/story/2014/06/yes-nixon-scuttled-the-vietnam-peace-talks-107623/

Henry Kissinger, America's Most Notorious War Criminal, Dies At 100
https://www.huffpost.com/entry/henry-kissinger-dies_n_6376933ae4b0afce046cb44f?
email_hash=ed5055bf6ae3689520b2db35a8e2fd5f989427a4

The "Socialists"

After reading the first few chapters, it probably doesn't seem like there was much left to ruin if the title of this book is to be taken seriously. But somewhere, sometime around the start of the 20th century, people started thinking, "Hey, what if we took the words of our famous founders and presidents literally? What if all men ARE created equal? What if Lincoln was right and we are a government of the people, by the people and for the people?" Maybe it was Susan B. Anthony in her fight for women's suffrage. Maybe it was W. E. B. Dubois in his fight for equal rights for African Americans when he said, "There is in this world no such force as the force of a person determined to rise." Or maybe it was someone we've never heard of who inspired others with their deeds. Wherever the first spark of illumination came from, it coalesced into a feeling that America could become an ideal that the world could look to and aspire to become. Four presidents in the 20th century recognized this potential that was instilled in our Declaration and Constitution and the words of Lincoln, and decided that the United States should become "a thousand points of light" as George H. W. Bush once projected in his most famous speech. Unfortunately, he wasn't one of the four.

Two provided the policy framework: Franklin Roosevelt and Lyndon Johnson. Two others provided the inspiration and thoughtfulness: John Kennedy and Jimmy Carter.

Granted, all were Democrats, and for that reason, and that reason alone many will dismiss what I am about to show. However, in the interest of this book, their party is utterly irrelevant. Every president had faults, failures and triumphs. Well, most of them had the first two. I'm a fan of Teddy Roosevelt, a Republican who understood the value of our natural resources and reigned in abusive corporate power. I also have an intense loathing for Woodrow Wilson and Grover Cleveland, both Democrats: one, a virulent racist who ordered the re-segregation of the federal government; the other, a rapist and an aggressively "free-market" policymaker.

The problem with assessing any presidency is that more often than we'd like, we won't know the true impact of their policies until much later, sometimes decades. And there's also the difficulty of weighing the choices they had to make to move their agenda forward. For example, for FDR to enact his New Deal, he had to court the votes of Southern Democrats who supported racist laws and policies. So to help most of America during the Depression, he calculated that a significant portion must be left wanting. To her credit, First Lady Eleanor Roosevelt didn't see it that way and became an outspoken advocate for civil rights during and after FDR's presidency. And don't get me started on Manzanar and the racist policy of putting Japanese Americans in concentration camps. That's Jackson-level obscene. So I completely understand if someone holds a grudge against him for that reason.

However, it's hard to dispute FDR's impact in the 20th century. Before his presidency, the US was one of the great powers in the world; after his presidency, the US was THE great power in the world. Not only did he navigate the country through the Great Depression and World War 2, but he established safety net agencies that reduced the amount of wealth that could be stolen from the poor and middle class, as well as secured at least a modest living standard for the aged, many of whom would have previously faced a life of destitution at the end of their lives. These agencies included the Social Security Administration, FDIC, FHA, and the SEC, as well as two agencies specifically designed to help the farmers who had been grossly neglected under the previous three administrations. In 1938, he added the Food, Drug and Cosmetics Act which gave the FDA authority to establish regulations and testing for food and drug safety for the first time in our history. The New Deal was instrumental in the

US becoming the preeminent world power of the 20th century. FDR did all of this having to horse trade with racist Southern Democrats on one side, and corporate Republicans hell-bent on destroying those same safety nets on the other. Obama is the only president in the last century who faced a Congress that was less willing to work with him.

I would argue that had it not been for World War 2, Social Security and the other agencies that had stopped the cycles of economic booms and busts would have been whittled down or dismantled out of spite, if for no other reason. That's how much corporate America and the wealthy hated him. During a war, however, it would have been political suicide to advocate taking away those programs. By the time the war ended, people had grown accustomed to the feeling of security for a decade. There was no taking them away.

It was not met without resistance, however.

"Despise" is not too strong a word for how the moneyed interests felt about FDR. He was one of their own after all - coming from a very wealthy family - yet he was helping the poor. In their eyes, he was a traitor to their class. They worked against him and took every opportunity to advocate a reversal of his policies. They claimed that the New Deal plus his anti-trust threats beginning in 1935 had made the economy unfriendly to business. Their calls to curb government spending on his public work programs (which robbed them of cheap labor) began to gain traction with the public as did their message regarding the evils of deficit spending. Never mind that deficit spending is exactly what businesses do all the time, especially when they are start-ups. So to pacify their whinging, FDR pulled back on federal spending. The result was the recession of 1937. Unemployment, which had been reduced from 25% when he took office down to 14%, spiked to 19%, and GDP growth sank from a robust 5% per year to -3%. FDR responded with a 5 billion dollar federal program designed to increase purchasing power, and in one of his fireside chats offered that it was "the job of the government to create economic upturns". In 1939, he added the Lend Lease Act, which authorized increased government spending on defense to help the Allies in Europe without actually involving us in the war. Not only did this help the economy and give strength to Britain and Russia in their fight against the Nazis but it also put the country in a much better position to fight the war once it was drawn into it.

The wealthy didn't stop there in their efforts to sabotage FDR's programs. That had been their Plan B. Their Plan A was to literally overthrow Roosevelt in 1933 with the Business Plot (also known as the Wall Street Putsch, in reference to Hitler's Bierhall Putsch). The scheme was hatched by a group of businessmen and bankers to install retired Marine General Smedley Butler as a puppet dictator for their interests. Twice awarded the Medal of Honor and the most decorated marine in US History, Butler listened to their plan, then promptly reported them to Congress. What is interesting is that's all that came of it. No official inquiry, no public committee hearings. The individuals named in the plot all denied being part of it. Several of the plotters owned newspapers. Some owned the banks that financed others. So it shouldn't be a surprise that much of the major media began to suggest that the plot was all some hoax. Still, in 1935, Smedley was quoted as saying:

"I spent 33 years and four months in active service as a member of our country's most agile military force – the Marine Corps. I served in all commissioned ranks from a second lieutenant to Major-General. And during that period I spent most of my time being a high-class muscle man for Big Business, for Wall Street, and for the bankers."

At the onset of World War 2, Roosevelt created the National War Labor Board to negotiate any settlements necessary between workers' unions and companies that provided war materials and machinery. He was concerned that protracted disputes and shutdowns might cripple the war effort. Sewell Avery was the CEO of retailing giant Montgomery Ward, which provided everything from clothes to tractor parts. He was rabidly anti-New Deal and anti-worker, a prominent member of several right-wing business groups, and had been a participant in the Wall Street Putsch. After Avery refused to comply with three separate collective bargaining agreements (and again, it can't be stressed enough that these were labor contracts that he had already agreed to, but was now refusing to abide by), Roosevelt signed an executive order to seize Montgomery Ward under the War Labor Disputes Act. First, the government seized Ward's Chicago headquarters. Then it seized its facilities in six states. The episode reached a climax when FDR ordered the National Guard to physically remove Avery from his office. There was some public backlash – majority sentiment felt that FDR had overstepped – and several lawsuits filed by Avery but he ultimately lost every one. Even though Roosevelt was always reluctant to use these powers, on more than forty occasions during the war he was forced to seize companies until they agreed to comply with their own labor agreements. Several Presidents have since enacted the War Powers Act to achieve quick responses to threats but none have been forced to do so as often to protect actual national security.

Lyndon Johnson expanded FDR's vision of helping the less fortunate with his own: the Civil Rights Act and the Great Society programs of Medicare and Medicaid. However, his legacy will always be tied to the policy and strategic failures of Vietnam. His failure there was catastrophic in large part because he listened to people who were still fighting World War 2. It cost his party both the election in 1968 as well as the affection of one of his mistresses. Still, the introduction of Medicare and Medicaid in addition to the freedoms guaranteed by the Civil Rights Act have been central to the identity of the United States for the last 60+ years.

Still, Reagan and every significant conservative leader of the last half-century believed and still believes that these programs are Americanized socialism: spending government money to help people who couldn't help themselves. Newsflash:

they are but that doesn't make them any less valuable or important to our national identity or our economy. It's much cheaper to help people out of a difficult situation than it is to leave them to desperate measures. That point shouldn't be controversial. But as much as conservatives hate Social Security and other entitlements, they don't hesitate to borrow from their funds. In April of 1983, Reagan became the first of several Presidents to dip into Social Security funds to cover the costs of his government spending.

What is perhaps the most interesting aspect of the presidencies of FDR and LBJ is that their terms as President yielded the highest GDPs of the 20th century. So in addition to making America a better place to live, they also made it a more profitable place to work. Sure, government spending is a factor in GDP, but that spending also lays a better foundation for private enterprise. Private enterprise thrives in the US because the federal government created a vast infrastructure network that facilitates the transportation of goods, one of the best higher education systems, and one of the best support systems for research in the world. Nearly one-half of all basic scientific research is either produced or funded by the US federal government. That research is passed on for pennies on the dollar to private enterprise.

NASA is a perfect example. If NASA was a privately owned company that held the patents to everything they funded or researched, the market valuation for it conservatively would be many times more than any current company. Apple is the most valuable, currently valued at $2.54 trillion in market capitalization, which essentially is what the stock market thinks it's worth. But Apple didn't invent smoke detectors, MRI, CAT Scans, cordless tools, about a thousand new applications for Teflon, Velcro, and Mylar, or innovations in heating, cooling, lightweight materials, and insulation. NASA did. Most lightweight weather gear and nearly every athletic shoe produced in the last 20 years was produced using NASA-developed tech. Sixty percent of the computer chip market in the 1960s was purchased by the federal government, much of that by NASA. Without that investment, we still might not have home computers or smartphones because it would have taken decades to develop if it were left solely to the public consumer market. The companies that "invented" these technologies were in large part driven by government investment and a primary driver in that effort was NASA. One could literally spend an hour noting the benefits to the US and humanity in general from the Apollo program alone.

Which brings us to LBJ's predecessor, John Kennedy. It was his vision to make NASA a centerpiece of American pride and technological innovation. And although he would never see its greatest triumph, landing on the moon in the same decade he famously tasked America with his vision, his enthusiasm for the program inspired the hundreds of thousands of people who involved themselves in the project.

He had that same enthusiasm for a world vision for peace. It wasn't just the Peace Corps. It was in his foreign policy. Many times he was goaded into starting a war with the Soviets by his military advisors and more conservative politicos, but each time he chose the path of negotiation. His decision not to support the Bay of Pigs invasion, something that had been concocted to force him into war with Cuba, ultimately resulted in an exchange of $53 million in medical supplies with Cuba for many of the captured Cuban exiles who participated in the invasion. Castro noted in an interview in 1963 with a French journalist that both he and Khrushchev felt Kennedy was someone they could negotiate with. This was proven again with his handling of the Cuban Missile Crisis, where on its face he put forth a tough guy posture, but resolved the conflict peacefully with backroom negotiating, trading missiles from Cuba for missiles from Turkey. Kennedy was also quite hesitant to support an extremely corrupt regime in South Vietnam with a commitment of US troops, something Johnson did and later regretted. Kennedy sought to make peace with the world rather than try to dominate and control it. That, more than anything, was probably what got him assassinated.

Jimmy Carter was elected in 1976 largely due to backlash against the Nixon/Ford Watergate debacle. People were tired of the lying and the adversarial attitude the Republicans had with the press, the anti-war protesters, and pretty much anyone who wasn't Republican. For better or worse, Carter brought an air of honesty to the White House. He lacked the guile of most Presidents which did not help him when it came to public relations, but he had more vision than most. His policies were designed specifically to help the under-served and opened the doors to true democratization. If you're looking for a president who governed during a time of highest GDP (Carter is 3rd behind FDR and LBJ), expansion of infrastructure, and laying a groundwork for the future, then Carter is your guy.

He embraced more logical aspects of neoliberalism. Not everything needed to be regulated by the federal government. For example, he was the one who first decided that oil prices didn't need to be federally controlled. In 1973, OPEC implemented an embargo against countries that had supported Israel in the Yom Kippur War, the US under Nixon being one of them. So in addition to the widespread belief that the world was running out of oil, Carter reasoned that leaving that limited supply in control of capricious OPEC nations was a national security concern. So he untethered US oil prices from government regulation, cautioned that the US needed to free itself from foreign influences on energy, and created the Department of Energy to oversee a comprehensive plan for nuclear, solar, wind, and other energy sources. OPEC responded by dropping production from nearly six million barrels per day to under four million barrels per day practically overnight. Gas prices skyrocketed and long lines of cars waiting at gas stations due to shortages soured Americans on energy independence. However, the price fluctuations that benefited the American economy over the subsequent decade would not have been possible without Carter's deregulation.

And while oil prices don't control the economy, they certainly have a huge impact. From the end of World War 2 until

1974 oil prices remained consistently between $20 - $25 per barrel (inflation adjusted). That was the largest sustained period of economic growth in American history. I realize that also coincides with the American economy being the only modern economy in the world that wasn't devastated by World War 2, which essentially gave American goods a worldwide monopoly for nearly three decades, but it certainly helped that oil prices were relatively cheap and stable. That changed in 1973 when OPEC first decided to exert its influence on the world by choking off the flow of Mideast oil. The price shot up to $43. It eventually went up to around $50 and remained there for the next five years. In 1979, economic stagnation and inflation (cleverly called "stagflation" in the media) was driven by OPEC's decision to drop production forcing oil prices to jump again to $78 per barrel. It only got worse the following year when oil prices peaked at $104. Carter's response to shift America's energy consumption away from oil and more towards coal, natural gas, and nuclear energy, as well as to invest in alternative energies like solar, reduced our dependence on Middle East oil by 23%. Unfortunately, he wasn't around long enough to enjoy the cost savings. That policy was reversed under Reagan. Now forty years, three wars and one horrific terrorist attack later, we finally seem to be coming to the same conclusion Carter did: that depending on oil from the Middle East is a trap. Well, some of us, anyway.

  As for the price of oil and its impact on the Reagan economy, for the first few years of his administration, Saudi Arabia tried to choke back production due to the decreased demand that Carter had caused. The Soviet Union took advantage of the opportunity by increasing their production to fund their incursion into Afghanistan. Whether it was due to ideological reasons (Afghanistan, like Saudi Arabia, is primarily Shia Muslim) or economic reasons (the USSR was encroaching on Saudi Arabia's market share), the Saudis then glutted the market causing oil prices to crater. That achieved two unintended consequences: it strained the economy of the USSR to the breaking point and it boosted the economy of the US. Reagan is often given credit for these developments, but the fact is that they would have happened even if Bonzo was President. Militarily, the Soviet failure in Afghanistan was far more due to the black budget funding efforts of Congressional Democrats like Charlie Wilson than anything Reagan did.

Among other forward-thinking policies Carter was responsible for was the deregulation of the trucking industry. Companies like DHL, UPS, and Federal Express (now known as FedEx) went from small delivery companies to multinational giants in less than a decade. Combined those companies' revenue in 1980 was less than $250 million. Today it's roughly $300 billion, and the trucking industry as a whole generates more than $875 billion in earnings. Carter also deregulated railways allowing them to compete by increasing the incentive to ship by rail. The American Consumer Institute concluded that from 1980 – 2020, accounting for inflation, the industry's productivity increased 159%, shipping volumes increased 57%, and prices plummeted 44%. All of these things conservatives claim Reagan was responsible for, but in fact, it was Carter.

He also understood that information was likely to be the deciding factor in global politics, so he deregulated communication, which allowed for the commercial development of the Internet. The US Postal Service began looking into offering an email service in 1977 called E-COM. A company called Compuserve began offering interoffice email in 1978. In addition, new phone companies offering long-distance service sprouted up and the race toward cheaper communication was on. Today's smartphones would not have been possible without Carter's policies.

Given the exponential growth of the shipping and communication industries, without Carter's deregulation, internet commerce would still be confined to the realm of science fiction. Was he so visionary that he knew his actions would bring about this inevitable result? Maybe, maybe not. He certainly understood that by deregulating them it would increase competition. One way to get an edge on the competition is innovation and innovation is often nothing more than combining two seemingly disparate things to make a new one. He was indisputably a smart guy, having studied nuclear engineering, so it's not a stretch.

He signed the Airline Deregulation Act of 1978 which made air travel affordable and accessible for every American. Whereas less than 30% of the public had flown commercially in 1976, 60% of Americans were booking at least one round-trip flight per year by 2000. He also eliminated the last of the Prohibition laws which had outlawed nationwide transport of alcohol as well as home brewing. So without Carter, we would not have any of the microbrews we currently enjoy, and we would have likely been subjected to at least twenty Smokey and the Bandit sequels. His contribution to good taste can not be underestimated.

But just as important as his deregulation, Carter put some muscle back into the regulatory agencies, specifically the Federal Trade Commission, which had atrophied under the previous two presidents. For example, it was the FTC under Carter that successfully established safety standards for cars. So effective were his regulators that the sugar, oil, and broadcast industries successfully lobbied members of Congress to try to have the agency shut down and/or completely defunded. It marked the first time a federal agency had ever been shut down (if only for a few days) but ever since Republicans have used that as precedent to threaten government shutdowns over funding.

Among the domestic government programs Carter initiated was the Superfund which has been responsible for cleaning up 347 toxic waste sites nationwide largely at the expense of the original polluters. As far as defense spending, he directed the creation of DEVGRU (aka Seal Team Six) after the military failed to rescue the Tehran hostages. Carter oversaw the deployment of the first E-3 AWACS (a system that has been a critical part of coordinating our armed forces for the last four decades) and the cruise missile program (the Navy's Tomahawk and the Air Forces AGM-86A). He canceled the B-1 bomber, in large part because it was a pointless program: the plane carries half the payload of the B-52, its operational range is 1,000 miles less, has a much lower ready rate, is not nuclear capable and can not drop its bombs at supersonic speeds (its primary reputed advantage over the B-52). There's a good reason B-52s are still in service today. By the way, Reagan re-started the B-1 program at a cost of $283 million per plane. He built 100 of them. Carter started the B-2 stealth project, poured funding into the F-117 stealth fighter, and gave the go-ahead for the first Trident missile submarines.

He also withdrew US military support for despots like Samoza in Nicaragua, the Shah in Iran, and Marcos in the Philippines. If the US was going to claim that its goal was to spread democracy and freedom around the world, Carter was going to make sure that we at least backed up that claim by not supporting dictators. He also negotiated peace between Israel and Egypt, who had been at war for more than a decade. In short, had Carter remained president, there's a very good chance that your house would be solar-powered, your car would be electric and your kids would not have to worry about terrorism.

Carter also predicted the crisis of identity that undermines the great intentions our nation was founded on:

"Too many of us now tend to worship self-indulgence and consumption. Human identity is no longer defined by what one does, but by what one owns. But we've discovered that owning things and consuming things does not satisfy our longing for meaning... You see every extreme position defended to the last vote, almost to the last breath by one unyielding group or another. You often see a balanced and fair approach that demands sacrifice, a little sacrifice from everyone, abandoned like an orphan without support and without friends... We have lost our way ... because we have exalted 'a mistaken idea of freedom'; our self-indulgence has led us to assert every right as absolute, every form of compromise or regulation as inimical to freedom, and ... to elevate the very avatar of self-absorption to the highest office in the land."

This was called his "malaise" speech, but it rings more true today than when he first uttered it almost forty-five years ago.

So why is Carter's presidency incorrectly regarded by so many as a failure? Primarily it is for one reason and one reason only: he committed the cardinal sin in America of telling the truth.

I have friends, family, and acquaintances in Canada, Venezuela, Colombia, Brazil, Mexico, England, France, Italy, Spain, Poland, Germany, Finland, Romania, Russia, India, Japan, Korea, and Indonesia and I can tell you from that sample that no people on Earth hate being told the truth more than Americans. They will hate you for life if you tell them something that doesn't have a little sweetener to it. It's not particularly close, either. So when Carter told us about malaise, when he told us about the need to move from oil to more renewable sources of energy and that it might at first be uncomfortable but in the long run we'll be more prosperous, when he told us that he sometimes felt lust, when he told us anything that happened to be true, Americans hated him for it because it revealed our flaws and it showed us the flabby parts that needed work.

Reagan never did. He told us fairy tales and people loved that because the good guys always won and there was always a happy ending. The problem with fairy tales though is that while they are sometimes grounded in real life, they rarely tell the real story. As it turned out, Reagan was little more than a party clown, and the shreds of the popped balloons on the floor he left behind turned out to be choking hazards.

In 2010, CATO analyst Ivan Eland published a book called Recarving Rushmore, which ranked the presidents by how libertarian (read: working toward a smaller government) their administrations were. He ranked Jimmy Carter #8, right behind George Washington, largely on the strength of his de-regulating key strategic industries (airline, phone, trucking, railroad). Reagan, on the other hand, was ranked #34, two spots *below* noted liberal, government-growing Lyndon Johnson.

Woodrow Wilson was extremely racist — even by the standards of his time
https://www.vox.com/policy-and-politics/2015/11/20/9766896/woodrow-wilson-racist

Grover Cleveland's Sex Scandal: The Most Despicable in American Political History
https://www.thedailybeast.com/grover-clevelands-sex-scandal-the-most-despicable-in-american-political-history

The New Deal
https://www.history.com/topics/great-depression/new-deal

The New Deal Achievements
https://www.pbs.org/video/roosevelts-new-deal-acheivements/

Airports Built by the New Deal
https://livingnewdeal.org/new-deal-categories/infrastructure/airports/

Bridges and Tunnels Built by the New Deal
https://livingnewdeal.org/new-deal-categories/infrastructure/roads-bridges-tunnels/

The Plot Against American Democracy That Isn't Taught in Schools
https://www.rollingstone.com/politics/politics-features/coup-jan6-fdr-new-deal-business-plot-1276709/

Remembering the Montgomery Ward Seizure: FDR and War Production Powers
https://www.lawfareblog.com/remembering-montgomery-ward-seizure-fdr-and-war-production-powers

FDR seizes control of Montgomery Ward
https://www.history.com/this-day-in-history/fdr-seizes-control-of-montgomery-ward

Historic Presidential Affairs That Never Made it To the Tabloids
https://www.history.com/news/presidential-affairs-jfk-lbj-fdr-harding-clinton-trump

I Was With Fidel Castro When JFK Was Assassinated
https://newrepublic.com/article/120460/fidel-castro-reaction-kennedy-assassination-cuba

Crude Oil Prices - 70 Year Historical Chart
https://www.macrotrends.net/1369/crude-oil-price-history-chart

Global Surplus Crude Oil Production Capacity 1970–2021
https://www.eia.gov/international/content/analysis/special_topics/Global_Surplus_Crude_Oil_Production_Capacity/full-report.pdf

Jimmy Carter, Deregulator Extraordinaire
https://www.forbes.com/sites/briandomitrovic/2023/03/03/jimmy-carter-deregulator-extraordinaire/?sh=755a737555b7

History of Superfund
https://www.epa.gov/superfund/superfund-history-printable-version

FTC v. Carter, 464 F. Supp. 633 (D.D.C. 1979)
https://law.justia.com/cases/federal/district-courts/FSupp/464/633/1519890/

Michael Pertschuk, unyielding consumer watchdog, dies at 89
https://www.washingtonpost.com/obituaries/2022/11/18/michael-pertschuk-consumer-ftc-dead/

Brief History of Cruise Missiles
https://en.wikipedia.org/wiki/AGM-86_ALCM

Jimmy Carter Legacy
https://www.theguardian.com/world/2011/sep/11/president-jimmy-carter-interview

The "Main Street" Messiah

In Kennedy, the Democrats had a dynamic personality effectively projecting a world where people helped each other while striving to achieve high ideals and great technological advancements. He was willing to make agreements with the communists. He didn't have to overthrow them in favor of dictators who would be controlled with financial incentives. He had seen the horrors of war firsthand and correctly reasoned there must be a better way. Much of America felt the same as evidenced by his 70% approval rating throughout his Presidency, even through the fallout from the Bay of Pigs fiasco. But what they might not have known was that Kennedy, who had campaigned on the notion that the US was trailing the Soviets in the space race (which was true), also said that the US was trailing them on the number of nuclear armaments. This was not even remotely true. And while he talked about civil rights and other such lofty ideals, the reality is that it was Johnson who pushed them through. Kennedy dragged his feet on a number of these domestic initiatives. He was also fairly friendly to the wealthy, becoming the first president since the war to significantly lower their taxes. It was Kennedy who said that "a rising tide raises all boats", a mantra that Republicans to this day hold dear. Coming from a wealthy family, he understood that to get and do the other things, he had to throw them a bone.

What the Republicans and their benefactors wanted was someone who could be like Kennedy: someone who had charisma that could appeal to the common man and appear to have their best interests in mind while implementing the policies that would primarily benefit the wealthy.

Enter Ronald Reagan. Even during his acting career, he had been a corporate shill, doing commercials and other presentations for General Electric, Chesterfield and Lucky Strike cigarettes, Royal Crown (RC) Cola, Campbell Soups (specifically V8 drinks), the Cigar Institute of America (although he maintained that he smoked, but never inhaled), Westinghouse, Van Heusen, and the Union Pacific Railroad.

And like Nixon before him, he was a rabid anti-communist. In 1976, he failed in his bid to unseat incumbent Gerald Ford for the Republican nomination. Ford characterized him as "a superficial, disengaged, intellectual lazy showman who didn't do his homework and clung to a naive, unrealistic, dangerous worldview." Unfortunately for Jimmy Carter in 1980, the electorate didn't care. They didn't care that the world was complex and often nuanced with many valid points of view. They just wanted someone to tell them that America was #1 and that everything was very simple: greed was good, communism was bad, and that the business of America was business. It also helped Reagan that the hostage crisis in Iran hadn't been resolved. As Nixon had with Vietnam, several parties secretly negotiated with key players in Iran on Reagan's behalf to hold the hostages until after the election. It's amazing what one can buy abroad for a mere $40 million. Hours after he was inaugurated, they were released.

Meanwhile, the Soviet economy was catastrophically rife with corruption. An economy that had grown at a healthy pace during the 1950s and early 60s – in some years at a greater rate than that of the US - had slowed to a near standstill by the mid-1970s. Brezhnev's second central plan (1970-1975) was increasingly heavy on defense spending (between 12%-15% of the USSR's GDP) despite the fact they had no pressing need. Testing it is one reason an incursion into Afghanistan seemed like a promising opportunity. His plan also focused more on producing consumer goods rather than industrial capital goods. That was a huge mistake. Not only were Russian state-owned manufacturers trying to compete with the likes of Levi Straus making blue jeans and Rolex making fine watches, but in doing so they inadvertently flooded the market, meaning profit margins were meager for clearly inferior products. It's OK to have slim margins for a cheap product if you can sell millions of units, but it's a death sentence if you can't reach those numbers. And since failure to meet expectations in the Soviet Union carried a little more gravity than it did in the West (gulag, anyone?), it became commonplace for regional administrators to lie about making their quotas. This failing created a strong black market for Western goods, which further undermined confidence in Soviet leadership. The leaders also failed to recognize the upside of investing in the development of an emerging and what would prove to be decisive market: computers.

The USSR had a one-party government, with ministers and bureaucracies for each industry, with additional levels of ministers, each facing a quota for production set by the central plan. This allowed for scapegoating of lower-level administrators for failures, thereby insulating the ministers at the top. If you've ever tried to talk to tech support or your medical insurance company about a claim, you understand how this works in reality quite well. Calling customer support, regardless of the business, is often an exercise in futility due to the numerous layers of bureaucracy and specialization. What is certain is that you will never speak with anyone capable of changing company policy, or anyone who was involved in conceiving it. In the end, you'll likely have to fix the instigating issue yourself, probably by watching a how-to YouTube video while you attempt it. Nothing like do-it-yourself minor surgery. That was the entire Soviet economic system. The irony is that due to the recent consolidation of industries in the US, capitalism has likewise achieved that same level of stagnation and paralysis, only in our system, one guy at the top is making a billion dollars from it. Of course, Russia has billionaires too. But they got that way by being the primary beneficiaries of the black market opportunities before the

USSR fell, then buying up everyone else's shares of the formerly state-owned industries for pennies on the dollar after the fall.

The Chernobyl nuclear power plant in Pripyat, Ukraine is a perfect illustration of how the system worked. The man who was in charge of building it was not a nuclear engineer, but a bureaucrat who had been successful with other building projects. He was given a date to have it finished, then given limited resources to do so. As a result, he cut corners and used whatever materials were readily available to get the job done, like combining the containment buildings for reactors 3 & 4 (where the meltdown occurred) to save money. They used tar to weatherproof the roof of the building as if it were a house. The reactor itself had a known design flaw but no one bothered to fix it because it would have "cost too much". All of this compounded the problem when something inevitably went terribly wrong. There had been a less severe accident with one of the flawed reactors at another plant near St. Petersburg a few years earlier, but the mishap had been effectively covered up by the KGB to preserve the notion that all was well. The area around Pripyat, now called the Chernobyl Exclusion Zone, covers roughly a thousand square miles and is still highly radioactive to this day. There is a birth defect common in Ukraine and Belarus called 'Chernobyl heart' specifically caused by the radiation poisoning of that area.

In purely business terms, it turns out that the Soviet empire wasn't so much brought down by American exceptionalism as it was plain, old-fashioned incompetence and greed. To be fair, their version of greed was less about the money and much more about not being imprisoned.

Politically, what brought the USSR down in 1991 was a reluctance to use military force to quell demonstrations and subsequent insurrections. Previously, troops had been sent into Georgia in 1924, East Germany in 1953, Georgia and Hungary in 1956, and Czechoslovakia in 1968 to subdue protests against Soviet policy. Brezhnev had reconsidered the effectiveness of military interventionism after the 1968 Prague uprising and signed onto the Helsinki Accords in 1975. Thirty-five nations, including the US, the USSR, and much of Europe agreed to the treaty which promised to refrain from using military force against such protests. Gorbachev and his Minister of Foreign Affairs Eduard Shevardnadze proved their commitment to it by refusing to use military force to quiet a series of demonstrations that began in Poland in 1989 and then spread to East Germany, Czechoslovakia, Hungary, Bulgaria, and Romania. The floodgates of revolutionary reform in the Eastern Bloc had been opened.

The war in Afghanistan was also a disaster. The Soviet occupation originally intended to provide support for an unpopular communist government that had taken power in 1978 via a military coup. By the early 1980s, that support was faltering. Gorbachev's Glasnost (meaning 'transparency') policy meant that people were now told the truth about how things were going instead of being fed their previous diet of state-run propaganda. They also knew that Gorbachev wasn't going to kill them if they made their displeasure known.

Russia on its own covers eleven time zones. The Soviet Union encompassed fifteen nation-states. That is a huge variety of peoples and cultures. It's not quite as many as there are in the US but that's a lot of cultural ideologies to accommodate. Given that their identities and grievances had been suppressed for half a century, a military misadventure in a zealously religious backwater proved to be the match that lit the fuse for radical change.

Conservatives like to claim that Reagan's defense spending, particularly SDI, forced the Soviets to increase their defense spending past critical levels. While the USSR did put a much greater percentage of its GDP into the military than the US, it had been doing so for 50 years. The upswing in spending had begun in 1970, not 1980. In fact, in 1989 Gorbachev revealed that the Soviet military budget was only $129 billion that year, half of what defense and intelligence analysts had projected, and that the

Soviet military budget had been decreasing for several years. They were not spending outrageous sums to counter Reagan's escalated defense spending; the blame for the economic collapse lay squarely with Brezhnev's administration, both in concept and execution and the increasing cultural unrest in the satellite countries.

Economically, the fall came from pressures that began in the South. To offset the added expense of the military conflict in Afghanistan, the Soviets increased the amount of oil they produced for export. After the Saudis glutted the market in response, Russian oil was greatly devalued on the world markets. The price of a barrel had dropped 75% (inflation-adjusted) from its high in 1980. Imagine how the current US economy would react if gas prices dropped from nearly $4 per gallon down to $1 per gallon. The costs of transportation and packaging, and even the price of many products themselves, like clothes and medicines that have ties to the oil industry, would likewise plummet, depending on how "free" the markets were. We might also see record profits from the companies that made them, exactly what happened in the 1980s and 1990s.

Ironically, had Reagan actually been the genius at fighting communism that he is lauded to be, he would have realized that continuing Carter's cutback of US oil consumption (decrease demand = decrease the price) would have driven the price of oil down even faster, thus speeding up the economic collapse of the Soviet Union. He could have led the Green Revolution *and* seen the Berlin Wall come down simultaneously *during* his administration.

So what was all the noise really about? One of the things that often gets overlooked in these discussions is that the Soviet Union's satellite countries played a crucial role in their economy. Cuba, for example, was their primary supplier of sugar. The Ukraine was a significant supplier of grains. Germany and Poland were and still are among the top producers of beef in Europe. Azerbaijan has one of the oldest and richest oil fields in the world. As mentioned before, the USSR, specifically Russia, committed a significant portion of its economy to its military might. That meant making and exporting weapons, mostly to satellite and allied countries. They topped the list of the world's most prolific arms exporters for more than half of the years from 1950-1980. In fact over that period, they exported nearly $306 billion in weapons and small arms around the world, $12 billion more than the US over the same time frame. In short, Reagan was mad that they were outselling the US in weapons. This had always been about business. In every year Reagan was in office, the USSR sold more weapons worldwide than the US. However, Gorbachev was not lying. From 1980 to 1988, their arms sales decreased by 31%. By the time the USSR finally collapsed, Russia accounted for less than half of the USSR's total arms sales. When Reagan took office, the US was responsible for 23% of the worldwide market in weapons sales. That has since grown to 41% by 2022. Currently, Saudi Arabia accounts for 24% of those US sales. And who have been the primary beneficiaries of this largess? It hasn't been the soldiers, marines, sailors, and airmen who continue to sacrifice their lives and well-being in a seemingly never-ending list of conflicts. Spending on healthcare for veterans remained relatively flat until 9/11, and since then the biggest driver of increased spending on the actual people has been housing allowances. However, five of the top six weapons manufacturers worldwide are American: Lockheed Martin, RTX, Northrup Grumman, Boeing, and General Dynamics, accounting for nearly $200 billion in annual revenue.

  So what did Reagan do for the domestic economy other than give loads of money to defense contractors? Well, despite being the guy who talked up Milton Friedman's ideas about how much healthier the economy would be with a smaller government, he actually increased the federal payroll by almost 250,000 non-military employees and increased government spending by 40%. Those developments sound oddly Keynesian which is the exact opposite of what Friedman and Reagan advocated publicly. Unemployment increased from 7.1% to a high of 9.8% during his first term, but was down to 7.5% by the re-election, but still higher than when he entered office. It continued to drop as oil prices went down in his second term.

Some have argued that the changes in the tax rate under Reagan are what spurred the economy on, but since he raised taxes a half dozen times in his two terms along with his famous tax rate cuts, about the only thing that can definitively be proved is that those on the upper end of the income spectrum were the primary beneficiaries of the tax changes. His spending tripled public debt and he became the first president to not raise the minimum wage since it was established in 1938.

He cut Social Security payouts by $2.3 billion while increasing Social Security tax by $2.7 trillion in 1983. The burden of the payout cut was placed on, as an example, high school seniors who were depending on those benefits to pay for college because their parents had either died or had become disabled. So in the spring of 1983, high school seniors dealing with the challenges of suddenly having only one parent had a choice: be enrolled full-time in college by April 1, 1983 (still in the middle of the school year) to keep their benefits and do both full-time high school and college workloads at the same time, or simply finish high school and forfeit all Social Security benefits along with any hope of attending college. As a further cost-cutting measure, Reagan ordered the Social Security Administration not to directly notify the 150,000 students who would be affected, citing it would be very expensive to send out individual notices. The high school guidance counselors were the ones saddled with delivering the bad news. He also began taxing Social Security payments as income for the first time in the program's history. As for the increased revenue? It never found its way into the fund. Instead, it was used to fund tax cuts for the rich.

But it's not like he cared. Reagan had been very vocal in his opposition to the idea of Social Security or any safety net program. He called unemployment insurance "a prepaid vacation plan for freeloaders," and welfare recipients were "a faceless mass waiting for handouts." He even went so far as to derisively call the progressive income tax which was largely responsible for establishing a middle class the "brainchild of Karl Marx."

Reagan is often credited with getting runaway inflation under control but the author of that solution was none other than Carter-appointed Fed Chairman Paul Volcker. All Reagan had to do was listen to the man. Interestingly enough, Reagan eventually fired Volcker because he didn't feel he was de-regulating the financial markets enough. In 1981, he further deregulated the savings and loan industry (which had initially been deregulated under Carter so that they could more effectively compete with banks) but then turned a blind eye to the fraud and corruption it enabled. The result was a systemic failure costing taxpayers close to $300 billion in bailouts. In Volcker's place, he appointed Alan Greenspan, who turned out to be one of the major enablers of the dot com bubble crash in the late 90s. Having already served as an economic advisor to both Nixon and Ford, Greenspan didn't think REMICs (a real estate investment vehicle created by Reagan's Tax Reform Act of 1986 that pooled mortgages and issued interests in themselves) were a dangerous creation. They turned out to be the primary driver of the Subprime Mortgage Crisis in 2007-2008 costing taxpayers an additional $2.223 trillion in bailouts. Reagan's point man on economic issues, David Stockman, famously claimed that government spending deficits have almost no consequences. That certainly didn't age well.

Reagan embraced the theory of the Laffer Curve, citing that the more you cut taxes, the more revenue the government gets, which can be true if the tax burden is onerous. However, they never quite fully grasped that it's a curve, meaning eventually there's a point where the revenue from lowering taxes yields diminishing returns. It's pretty clear we're now long past that point.

Reagan loved to say that governments only get in the way of private enterprise. He often cited Nobel Prize-winning economist Milton Friedman's notions about the power of free markets, known as "neoliberalism". One of the most common examples "free market" folks use to support his theories was the Chilean economy under General Augusto Pinochet. After he wrested power from Salvador Allende (mentioned earlier here among the CIA-sponsored coups) in 1973, Pinochet fully embraced Freidman's ideas. He privatized almost all industries (defense was obviously exempted) and it was that decision that supposedly turned his third-world economy into a powerhouse. It was no secret that Pinochet was a murderous tyrant and it was because of his ability to instill fear of imprisonment or death that he was able to implement the philosophy unilaterally. Any opposition literally disappeared. Estimates range from 3000 victims to as many as 30,000. What is not as well known is that by several economic indicators, the Chilean economy under him was no stronger than any other in South America. When he was finally deposed, Chile had more foreign debt than any country in South America. What is even less well-known is the fact that Chile's copper industry was never privatized. It was so vital to the Chilean economy that Pinochet never risked letting anyone else run it. How vital? That single industry supplied 30% of the government's revenue. To give some perspective to how huge a number that is, the total of *all* corporate taxes as a percentage of federal revenue in the US has hovered between 7% and 9% over the last decade. Even during the 1950s when taxes were at their highest levels of the century they averaged 28% of all federal revenues. Chile's government was getting that and more from one single entity.

It hasn't worked that well here, either. Corporate profits were at an all-time high last year, so why are so many companies cutting 10% of their workforce?

For the full story, we have to go back to the 1920s when companies made an effort to provide profit-sharing, healthcare, education, and retirement benefits. This was known as 'welfare capitalism'. It was a way they could attract the most highly qualified candidates to work for them. In fact, the CEO of

General Electric, Owen D. Young, gave a speech at Harvard Business School in 1927 denouncing businessmen who devised ways of "extracting every ounce of labor and every penny of compensation" and that businesses should think of their employees as humans rather than capital. It was a policy that worked for everyone. From 1948 to 1979, growth and worker pay matched productivity.

However, in 1981 Reagan named William Baxter, a former law professor at Stanford, as the Assistant Attorney General in charge of the Antitrust Division of the Department of Justice. He, like James Watt (the attorney Reagan appointed to lead the Department of the Interior despite his career of being openly hostile to environmentalism), was viewed as yet another appointee who had no interest in enforcing the laws he was delegated to enforce. His first action was to drop an antitrust suit against IBM, which he didn't think was a big deal because he felt that IBM was no longer the dominant force in computing. It clearly was. His second was settling the antitrust case against AT&T in exchange for the company breaking up into seven separate companies. No financial penalties for antitrust violations, just break up into smaller companies and we're good. Those two actions, along with Baxter's disdain for regulating mergers, signaled to big business that it was shopping season.

Enter Jack Welch. A General Electric engineer by trade, in 1968 he was promoted to general manager of developing a new type of plastic. His management style could best be described as "profit at all cost". He pushed the limit of working conditions and cut back on safety testing, and the result was an explosion that destroyed the factory. Fortunately, no one was hurt. The next day he was reprimanded by the board, but there were no further consequences. The same year Baxter was put in charge of antitrust (1981), Welch became CEO of GE. Previous CEOs had sought to maximize profit through research and development and by improving processes. To Jack, that was a waste of time and money; he wanted to extract value through accounting. Research and development were risky and expensive, whereas screwing over employees and customers was cheap and easy. Massive layoffs were a much more safe "and humane way" (his exact words) of maximizing profits. He developed a new system called "stack ranking" where he periodically fired the bottom 10% of employees based on productivity. This became an annual feature regardless of performance. During his first few years, Welch fired more than 100,000 people and closed a dozen factories. Welch claimed that what others had labeled as a 'brutal and cold' policy, that "what was truly brutal and false kindness was keeping people on payroll who weren't going to grow and prosper. There's no cruelty like waiting and telling people late in their careers that they don't belong… just when their job options are limited and they're putting their children through college or paying off big mortgages." Never mind that it was because of their productivity and loyalty that they got to the point where they could consider paying off a mortgage or putting their kid through college.

Welch also pioneered offshoring. "Ideally, you'd have every plant you own on a barge to move with currencies and changes in the economy". GE's first offshoring facility was in Gurgaon, just outside of Dehli, India. He started moving factories overseas and hiring temp workers in those countries to pay lower wages. In 1989, GE employed 277,000 workers in the US; by 2019, that number was 70,000. GE's manufacturing capability was a mere shell of its former self but that didn't matter because it had transferred the bulk of its business to financial services. By the time Welch retired, the company that Thomas Edison founded didn't even manufacture light bulbs. They outsourced production to a company in China and merely printed a GE label on them. Instead, its preferred business was to use its excellent AAA credit rating (as a manufacturer) to acquire loans to buy smaller businesses, something Baxter's laissez-faire position regarding vertical mergers encouraged.

In 1982, at the urging of Welch, Reagan accelerated the transition of the US economy from producing and manufacturing toward financing by legalizing another "free market" idea: stock buybacks. They allowed companies to use their profits to buy more stock. Regulated in the 1930s as a form of stock manipulation (and thus illegal), they don't create more jobs, increase wages, or grow the economy. They just make corporate execs and shareholders richer. It should not be at all surprising that the President who fired more than ten thousand air traffic controllers over improved pay and shorter hours could care less about worker wages, even though they were one of the few unions that had supported his election. Over the last 40 years, there has been a shift of more than $50 trillion from the bottom 90% to the top 1%. That's 50 with a "T", not a "B" or an "M". Remember when GOP congressmen were incessantly whining (generally during Democratic presidencies) about how the US doesn't manufacture anything anymore? Well, their guy Reagan is the reason why.

These big numbers get thrown around so much but it's hard to comprehend how big they truly are. If you were to count each second as it passed, it would take 11.5 days to count to one million. It would take 31.7 years to count to one billion and roughly 31,710 years to count to one trillion. This book has about 370,000 characters (including spaces), so a billion characters would equal about 2,700 copies of it. If you were to spend $100,000 per day, it would still take you 4,932 years to spend as much money as Elon Musk is currently worth. That means if you started on the same day the Egyptians broke ground building the Great Pyramid of Khufu at Giza, you still would have to spend for another three hundred years to spend it all. Thanks to the MegaPenny Project (coinsblog.ws/megapenny) you can get a visualization of what trillion pennies looks like. It would be a cube of stacked pennies nearly as wide as a football field. The US deficit is about $34 trillion; an adult human body has about 30 trillion cells. So when you hear on the news about a billion this or a trillion that, this might give help you understand how enormous these sums really are.

But I digress... Jack Welch's "innovations" forced competitors to employ similar strategies and now they are common practice, particularly in the tech sector. During his tenure, he bought back $10 billion worth of stock, closed factories, laid off thousands of workers, then claimed them as a loss on their taxes. In 2009, they finally paid a $50 *million* fine levied by the SEC for accounting fraud. In 2010, the company made $14.2 billion in revenue but paid $0 federal taxes because the bulk of the income, more than $9 billion, was offshore. In fact, they got a $3.2 billion refund because some of their products exploited a clean energy loophole. Hooray for capitalism!

Between 1979 and 2022 worker productivity went up nearly 65% but worker pay only went up 15% while CEO pay went up 1460%. As You Sow, a shareholder advocacy group publishes an annual survey of the 100 most overpaid CEOs. The list is compiled using a regression analysis comparing the CEO's yearly compensation to the company's financial performance returns to shareholders. Using their numbers, no CEO should be paid more than $15 million per year based on company performance, yet on average the top 100 are paid $33 million (an overpay of $18 million). In addition, the CEOs are paid 394 times more than their median worker. The AYS breakdown also listed what percentage of institutional investors (read: hedge funds) voted against the CEO current pay level. Only about 25% vote against what the CEO is getting paid. Why? Because those CEOs will then give a good portion of that overpay to those same hedge funds to further invest, thus raising the stock price, which they use to promote the idea that the CEO is doing a good job. This is precisely why stock buybacks were illegal before Reagan.

In 1979, 38% of all private sector workers had a pension. The year before Congress passed the Revenue Act, which allowed the creation of 401k plans. They were advertised as a tax shelter for additional income so that when someone retired, they would have three sources of income: Social Security, their pension, and whatever they had stashed away in their 401k. Under Reagan, the

IRS issued new rules allowing employees to contribute to them through salary deductions. Companies responded by switching their pension funds to 401k plans because they were cheaper to fund. That also put all that money in the hands of Wall Street. By the time Reagan left office, there was more than $300 billion invested in them. By the time the market crashed in 2008, $2.4 trillion had been invested. It was all gone. That didn't stop Wall Street managers from doling out more than $18 billion in performance bonuses.

And now we get to Reagan's foreign policy... In 1983, he sent the US Marines to Lebanon to restore order in the always turbulent Middle East. Instead of imposing order, their barracks was destroyed by a suicide bomber; 241 Marines lost their lives. Less than 48 hours later he ordered US forces to invade Grenada, a move that was criticized worldwide, including by staunch US allies Great Britain (imagine being castigated by your political doppleganger Margaret Thatcher, which is like being yelled at by your reflection in the mirror) and Canada.

A cynic might suggest the invasion was merely a diversion to the disaster in Lebanon. After all, the coup that had overturned the government in the former British territory had occurred almost two weeks before and not even the British cared enough to send troops. Grenadian PM Maurice Bishop along with seven others of his cabinet had been executed. Eventually, seventeen men in the Grenadian military were tried, convicted, and sentenced to prison for their participation. The bodies of the victims were never found, although stories have surfaced that there was an attempt to burn them (which failed). There is also photographic evidence of US soldiers helping to move the remains.

So could this have been yet another CIA coup?

Bishop had led a socialist revolution four years earlier and had successfully rebuilt the Grenadian economy into an emerging Caribbean powerhouse. While it's true he was friends with Fidel

Castro, he actively solicited diplomatic ties with every country in the vicinity including the US. He traveled to America to reset relations between the two countries, but the Reagan administration refused to meet with him at any cabinet level. Later it was revealed in a State Department memo that the administration felt that the revolution in Grenada led by Bishop was more dangerous than the revolutions in Cuba and Nicaragua because they spoke English in Grenada. When learning of this memo, Bishop commented during a speech in New York City that US reluctance to meet with him was also because the people of Grenada were predominantly black and that their struggle would appeal to 30 million black Americans. Black, socialist, and successful? Reagan and his backers could not have that in this hemisphere.

Does that sound too outrageous? Suggesting that Reagan was also possibly racist? Reagan had opposed both the Civil Rights Act of 1964 and the Voting Rights Act of 1965 and vetoed the Civil Rights Restoration Act in 1988 (but was overridden by Congress). In his second term as President, he actively sought to end Affirmative Action for all government contractors. Ironically, many of the largest companies in America objected to Reagan's effort, citing that profits and stock prices had benefited from the policy.

But if that's not enough evidence maybe this will tip the scales. A few years ago, the Reagan Library allowed public access to its audio files and one of them proved to be particularly interesting. It was a conversation between Reagan and Nixon regarding diplomats from African nations supporting a United Nations proposal from China. This is part of that transcript:

RONALD REAGAN: Last night, I tell you, to watch that thing on television as I did...

RICHARD NIXON: Yeah.

REAGAN: ...To see those monkeys from those African countries. Damn them. They're still uncomfortable wearing shoes.

NIXON: (Laughter) Well, and then they - the tail wags the dog there, doesn't it?

REAGAN: Yeah.

NIXON: The tail wags the dog.

Not to pile on, but during his campaign for president in 1980, he claimed our city streets were "jungle paths after dark", stressed states' rights (a dog whistle for segregationists), and decried welfare queens gaming the system. And did I mention where he kicked off that rhetoric in his campaign? Philadelphia Mississippi, where three civil rights workers had been murdered in 1964.

But back to Grenada... the US denies anything to do with Bishop's murder. Yet the US was the biggest beneficiary of getting rid of a rising socialist influence in Latin America, which concomitantly distracted the American public from the disaster of Reagan's strategy in Lebanon. During the same speech where he announced SDI, Reagan cautioned that the Grenadians were building an airport that the Russians and Cubans would use to launch long-range bombers. That, along with the safety of American medical students studying there, warranted military operations.

However, the "airbase" threat was utter nonsense. It takes that long of a runway to handle the kind of commercial airplanes necessary for international flights. Tourism was and still is the main industry in Grenada. Even during Reagan's tenure, the island had more visitors per year than residents. As many as 150,000 came from the US alone. What the island needed was an international airport that could handle the larger jets. It was what they were building and eventually built. By international agreement, the minimum length of runway for any such airport is 8000 feet. The most common length runs between 10000 and 12000 feet. All the things Reagan claimed were for military purposes were the same needs for international commercial airplanes.

What is incredibly ironic is that the main runway (labeled as "1/19") at National Airport is the busiest single runway in the country, handling 819 daily movements per day. It sits across the Potomac River from Washington DC and has since been renamed for Reagan. It is only 7169 feet long. The two other runways there - 15/33 and 4/22 – are 5,204 feet long and 5000 feet long respectively. Those are two of the shortest runways in the US and two of only a handful that are less than 6000 feet long. So in addition to the security complications of flying around DC, Reagan's airport has some of the busiest and shortest runways. It's a testament to the federal air traffic controllers who keep it running that dangerous incidents almost never happen. But it's also ironic that Reagan invaded a predominantly black country because its runway was too long, while the runway with his name on it in a predominantly white country is arguably too short. Sounds like a case of SDE. When the airport was completed, it was named for Bishop, not the country's "liberator".

The invasion was pitched as a resounding success to the American public by the administration and the media. And why not: an invasion force of more than 7,000 well-trained American soldiers faced down 1,500 poorly trained Grenadians and 700 Cubans. However, it was later revealed that many of the American casualties occurred because the soldiers had been directed using tourist maps that had no topography and all the critical locations marked by hand. The support fire had been directed using similar maps but due to minor differences in the hand-drawn coordinates, they had ended up firing on American positions. Those were some of the most tragic of the lapses of intelligence and logistics but perhaps not the most gobsmacking.

One of the most telling concerned the American medical students on the island. Assuring their safety was one of the primary reasons Reagan cited for the invasion. However, once the troops reached their objective and "liberated" the students, the soldiers were surprised to learn that there was another campus where even more American students were studying. Reagan and his invasion planners didn't even know that the school had two campuses. So it begs the question: how can a "rescue operation" being conducted in a foreign country not know who they are rescuing? For all the increased spending on defense, particularly weapons systems, did anyone in the Reagan administration consider that logistics might also be important? Or was any of what they claimed it was all about even a goal? Martine Powers' excellent investigative podcast for the Washington Post called "The Empty Grave of Comrade Bishop" details this and other anomalies regarding the invasion of Grenada.

One of the targets, a training camp at Calivigny, which coincidentally was where Bishop's body and those of his cabinet were reportedly taken after their execution, was bombed and shelled. Army Rangers were then ordered to take it from the Cubans who were stationed there. General Norman Schwartzkopf recalled that it was one of the stupidest missions he had ever heard of and that it had no tactical military value. However, if the mission was actually about destroying evidence, then maybe it did have value. The Rangers that were sent in did find decomposing bodies that had been unearthed and partially destroyed by the shelling. To this day, the Department of Defense, the State Department, the Defense Intelligence Agency, and the CIA refuse to comment on the action despite numerous FOIA requests and even inquiries by US lawmakers.

Three months later after Grenada, Reagan quietly withdrew the Marines from Lebanon. Osama bin Laden later cited *that withdrawal specifically* as a sign of American weakness. Am I blaming 9/11 on Reagan? Of course not, no more than I blame Richard Nixon for the emergence of Pablo Escobar. Bin Laden and Escobar were just the guys who saw opportunity where someone else had opened the door. In Reaganite terms, they were just taking advantage of a new free market.

How JFK's World View Shaped His Presidency
https://daily.jstor.org/how-jfks-world-view-shaped-his-presidency/

What happened when JFK lowered taxes?
https://www.back2facts.com/articles/2017/12/31/what-happened-when-jfk-lowered-taxes

14 Vintage Ads Featuring Ronald Reagan
https://www.mentalfloss.com/article/73588/14-vintage-ads-featuring-ronald-reagan

The Mysterious Case Of Danny Casolaro
https://www.grunge.com/1050700/the-mysterious-case-of-danny-casolaro/

The Thing We All Knew Finally Proved True: Reagan-Iran Edition
https://www.esquire.com/news-politics/politics/a43368900/reagan-iran-hostages/

More than 40 years later, a Texan reveals a secret that may have swayed an election
https://www.texasstandard.org/stories/ben-barnes-john-connally-iran-hostages-jimmy-carter-ronald-reagan-october-surprise/

Investigation into the Chernobyl Disaster
https://www-pub.iaea.org/MTCD/Publications/PDF/Pub913e_web.pdf

The Rise and Fall of Chile
https://www.washingtonpost.com/archive/business/1985/08/18/the-rise-and-fall-of-chile/0d3c8fc8-fb82-441a-b215-84b39156c5c2/

Chile's fiscal policy and mining revenue

https://www.afdb.org/fileadmin/uploads/afdb/Documents/Publications/anrc/CHILE_CASESTUDY_ENG__HR_PAGES.pdf

Bernie Sanders says tax share paid by corporations has fallen from 33% to 9% since 1952
http://www.politifact.com/truth-o-meter/statements/2014/aug/28/bernie-s/bernie-sanders-says-tax-share-paid-corporations-ha/

Crude Oil Prices in Inflation-Adjusted Terms
https://inflationdata.com/Inflation/Inflation_Rate/Historical_Oil_Prices_Chart.asp

The Sad Legacy of Ronald Reagan
https://mises.org/library/sad-legacy-ronald-reagan-0

Rumsfeld 'helped Iraq get chemical weapons'
http://www.dailymail.co.uk/news/article-153210/Rumsfeld-helped-Iraq-chemical-weapons.html

Ronald Reagan drew his reality from the films he watched, not from his aides or his briefing books.
http://articles.latimes.com/1991-04-28/opinion/op-1295_1_ronald-reagan/2

IS WILLIAM BAXTER ANTI-ANTITRUST?
https://www.nytimes.com/1981/10/18/business/is-william-baxter-anti-antitrust.html

W. F. Baxter, 69, Ex-Antitrust Chief, Obituary
https://www.nytimes.com/1998/12/02/business/w-f-baxter-69-ex-antitrust-chief-is-dead.html

How Jack Welch's Success Wrecked the Idea of the American Company
https://marker.medium.com/how-jack-welchs-success-wrecked-the-idea-of-the-american-company-eddc1bc05f78

The 100 Most Overpaid CEOs
https://www.asyousow.org/reports/the-100-most-overpaid-ceos

Inside the Mind of Osama Bin Laden
http://jime.ieej.or.jp/htm/extra/2001/09/13/20010922/wp-7.html

When Reagan tried to undo affirmative action, corporations fought back

https://www.washingtonpost.com/history/2024/01/21/ronald-reagan-affirmative-action-dei/

Historian Discusses Recording Of Reagan's Racist Comments Made To Nixon
https://www.npr.org/2019/07/31/747041525/historian-discusses-recording-of-reagans-racists-comments-made-to-nixon

'The Empty Grave of Comrade Bishop': Podcast episode guide
https://www.washingtonpost.com/investigations/2023/10/23/empty-grave-comrade-bishop-podcast-guide/

Laffer curve
https://en.wikipedia.org/wiki/Laffer_curve

The Progressive Income Tax in U.S. History
https://fee.org/articles/the-progressive-income-tax-in-us-history/

The Dangers of Buybacks: Mitigating Common Pitfalls
https://corpgov.law.harvard.edu/2020/10/23/the-dangers-of-buybacks-mitigating-common-pitfalls/

Ronald Reagan and The Great Social Security Heist
https://www.fedsmith.com/2013/10/11/ronald-reagan-and-the-great-social-security-heist/

How Four Decades of Tax Cuts Fueled Inequality
https://news.bloombergtax.com/daily-tax-report/how-four-decades-of-tax-cuts-fueled-inequality-james-b-steele

SIPRI Arms Transfers Database
https://www.sipri.org/databases/armstransfers

DEFENSE HEALTH PROGRAM 2021 Budget estimates
https://comptroller.defense.gov/Portals/45/Documents/defbudget/fy2021/budget_justification/pdfs/09_Defense_Health_Program/Defense_Health_Program_fy2021_Budget_Estimates.pdf

Trends in DoD's and VA's Budgets for Military Compensation
https://www.cbo.gov/system/files/2023-03/59013-Manpower.pdf

The Burning Bush

In the Old Testament, Moses was chosen by Yahweh to lead the Israelites out of Egypt and into Canaan. Evidently, God didn't care if people were living there already. Or that they were just different folks trying to get by and make a living. When God tells you to kill them all (including their livestock) and take their land, that's how the story usually goes down. And that's how it was told in the Bible, when Joshua, Moses' successor, took them into the land of milk and honey. However, science (specifically genetics) tells us that it didn't exactly go down that way. There's certainly destruction damage from the four Canaanite cities mentioned (although the damage at Jericho might have come from an earthquake), but the genetic evidence indicates that present-day Lebanese derive much of their genetic code from Canaanite ancestry. This conclusion was born from DNA evidence from the burial sites that predate the reported Israelite invasion by two centuries. This means that the Israelites may have invaded and bashed things up a bit, but they eventually co-existed and intermingled with the people Yahweh ordered them to annihilate.

All that to say is that when Reagan was "anointed" as the liberator of Eastern Europe when he told Gorbachev to tear "down that wall", he wasn't the one to see it through. George H. W. Bush was in office when it happened. But instead of doing what the Israelites and Canaanites did – work together to survive a harsh environment - Bush instead did a victory dance (or as kids today like to say, "flexed"), economist Francis Fukuyama famously declared the end of history and there was much rejoicing. Just not in Russia.

This was a case of the dog finally catching the car. For decades, conservatives had been banging the drum to destroy

Soviet communism, and when the fall finally came they didn't know what to do. Like most, Bush supported the reunification of Germany. But when it came to the independence movements of the Baltic states and the other satellite countries, to court favor with Gorbachev over the reunification of Germany he basically threatened to turn this car right around if they didn't behave. Chaos ensued with the US sitting back and doing nothing as these countries struggled to transition into largely privatized economies that created a cluster of oligarchs holding almost all of the resources. Many of the transitions were peaceful, but there were violent clashes in Azerbaijan, Georgia, and Armenia, and what was once Yugoslavia broke into six separate states that experienced a violent civil war and genocide. Romania was another Soviet Bloc country that underwent a violent transition with the overthrow of dictator Nicolae Ceaușescu, who ironically had been one of the few Communists who had reached out for Western help during the Cold War. Granted, not all of these occurred during Bush's administration, but all could have been mitigated had Bush wielded US influence more constructively.

So why didn't a President who had been Director of the CIA, Ambassador to China, and Vice President during the first stages of the thaw in the Cold War have a better plan for world peace? Could it have been that he realized that without Russia, he was going to have a hard time selling the American people on keeping up a defense budget that consumed 6% of our GDP ($321 billion, which is equivalent to almost $800 billion today) without an existential threat? Gorbachev had refused to use violence against his people where it had been the first go-to move under previous Russian leaders, and had ended the Russian war in Afghanistan. His successor, Boris Yeltsin, who wrested power after a failed coup against Gorbachev, was the Russian equivalent of W.C. Fields. To quote John LeCarre in The Russia House, "How the fuck do you peddle an arms race when the only asshole you've got to race against is yourself?" Well, maybe you just let the world go to hell in a handbasket and hope for a Bond villain to emerge.

Other than the START missile treaty, there were no trade agreements to help socialist economies transition into semi-capitalist ones. The problem, as always, is whenever a vacuum is created in the political arena, more often than not a bad actor comes to power. To put it another way, when the Soviet system failed, their economy was very much like our own during the Great Depression: in need of an infusion of capital to help distribute resources efficiently. Bush advocated the kind of response that Hoover had followed trying to minimize deficits, implementing austerity measures from the government in favor of unregulated neoliberal privatization. What they needed was a way to transition from Soviet governmental control toward Soviet governmental support, as FDR did with the New Deal. While several of the former Soviet states did fare better than they had under Soviet rule, they all underwent devastating recessions. And just like Germany after World War 1, when you have a bad economy and no help from the government, well, that situation rarely plays out well for anyone but the opportunist who seizes power. Again, Reagan's neoliberal playbook utterly failed at the one thing it purports to do: create opportunity for *all* through a free market.

No less than Richard Nixon understood the potential consequences of inaction in an op-ed he wrote for the New York Times in 1992. He maintained the same sentiments in a 1994 television interview:

"It is often said that the Cold War is over and the West has won it. That is only half true. Because what has happened is that the communists have been defeated but the ideas of freedom now are on trial. If they don't work there will be a reversion to not communism–which has failed–but what I call a new despotism, which would pose a mortal danger to the rest of the world. This is because it would be infected with the virus of Russian imperialism which of course has been a characteristic of Russian foreign policy for centuries. Therefore, the West has, the United States has, all those who want peace and freedom in the world, a great stake in freedom succeeding in Russia. If it succeeds it will be an example for others to follow, it will be an example for China to follow, and for the other communist states, the few that remain. If it fails, it means that the hardliners in China will get a new life. They will say that if it failed there, there is no reason for us to turn to democracy. That is part of what is at stake here."

In the 1992 op-ed, he had urged a new Marshall Plan for Eastern Europe, and if that course wasn't taken there would be wars throughout Europe, which turned out to be just more conservative fear-mongering. He did, however, correctly predict the rise of despotism driven by ideological hard-liners. What happened in Russia, though, was a consolidation of power from people who already had loads of it: political administrators and crime lords. Vladimir Putin was both.

One only needs to look at his time as mayor of St. Petersburg (technically, the Head of the Committee for External Relations in the Mayor's Office) to understand the man. In 1991, less than a year after he had been appointed, he was investigated for a deal in which $93 million in strategic metals were exchanged for food aid from neighboring countries to alleviate a famine caused by a brutal winter. The food never arrived and the money disappeared. During that same time frame, Bank Rossiya was founded by a consortium of Putin associates engaged primarily in the casino business whom Putin had given gambling licenses. The bank received a significant infusion of cash that year and since has been referred to by the US government as "Putin's cashbox". Adding another layer, many of the witnesses who were to testify in the investigation met untimely ends. All of this is detailed exceptionally well in Karen Dawisha's book, Putin's Kleptocracy.

Taking food from starving children to enrich his bank account not bad enough? How about starting a war by bombing your own people? Anna Politkovskaya was a journalist for Novaya Gazeta reporting on the brutal conflict in Chechnya. One of the stories she investigated was the 1999 apartment building bombing in Moscow that killed more than 300 civilians and acted as the primary trigger for the Second Chechen War. The device used was similar to one used in a bombing four days earlier in Buynaksk, Dagestan, a territory that borders Chechnya. Four days after the Moscow bombing, it was announced in the Russian Congress (the Duma) that a similar bombing had occurred in Volgodonsk, another city near Chechnya. Only it hadn't. That bombing didn't occur until three days after it had been announced. Chechen separatists were blamed for all three bombings. Yet another bomb was discovered a week later, only this time before it detonated in the border city of Ryazan. Putin praised the brave citizens who spotted the bomb, then immediately ordered the bombing of Grozny, the capital of Chechnya, in retaliation. The Second War in Chechnya had begun. Local police in Ryazan arrested three FSB agents and charged them with planting the bomb. The next day, the chief of the FSB claimed that the bomb in Ryazan was made of sugar and was only part of an anti-terror drill. He further ordered that the FSB agents be released. Politkovskaya's investigation revealed that Putin had likely been behind it all. Former FSB agent Alexander Litvinenko corroborated her accusation in two books about the FSB, the most explicitly detailed being Blowing Up Russia: Terror From Within. Putin, as prime minister, had used the terror attacks and his swift response to demonstrate that he was a better fit as leader of Russia than Yeltsin. Three months later, Yeltsin resigned and Putin was named President. Politkovskaya was later murdered in her apartment building (on Putin's birthday, no less) by contract killers. Litvinenko was famously poisoned in exile in England with polonium in his tea. Putin personally took charge of both of the investigations into their deaths. Needless to say, the person who ordered their deaths has yet to be revealed.

  Could Bush have prevented the rise of Putin? Putin came to power largely on the strength of his ties to Russian intelligence and the Russian underworld. In weak economies, people start looking for alternatives and often grasp onto the hope that a strong leader will lift them out of desperation. With a strong economy, it is much harder to sow fear and Bush could have played a key role in creating one in Russia. But like the Republicans that preceded him, Bush chose instead to gloat and take credit for something he had very little hand in precipitating, then did little if anything to forge positive trade relations. The Russian economy hemorrhaged. Gorbachev's successor, Boris Yeltsin, who is often portrayed as a boozy crazy uncle (and there is truth to that), but who was also the most Pro-Western Russian leader since Peter the Great, could not bluster his way to a stronger economic foundation. As a result, Russia and the world have been stuck with Putin since 1999.

Another act of neoliberalist ideology that didn't work out exactly as advertised was the North American Free Trade Agreement or NAFTA. Bill Clinton is often targeted for the blame of its failures but it was the elder Bush that shepherded it into law. It gave multinationals the opportunity to lower their labor costs without consequence in countries that did not share the US human rights ideals. It also allowed companies to abuse the territorial status of Guam and the Marshall Islands to claim their products were "Made in the USA", even though (because they are only territories) they were not subject to the same labor laws. Bush was all too happy to let corporations extract whatever value they could get from impoverished regions with the thought that he could get a healthy economy in return. As with any effort to put faith in Business America to act responsibly or to return value to the public from which they are stealing, this resulted in a crap economy for most people, thus almost assuring that he would be a one-term president.

Bush was also the author of the rise of the moron politician. His Vice President, Dan Quayle, was one of the most unimpressive VPs in history, both in terms of his accomplishments and his acumen. His troubles with facts, figures, and simple spelling are well-documented, but it was because his presence became acceptable in the White House that grossly uninformed hand puppets like Sarah Palin became palatable by their party. No one in their right mind previous to Bush would have allowed such a thing to occur. But Bush was desperate for a running mate with less charisma than a sock so he seemed more lively than a Chuck E. Cheese robot by comparison. So we got stuck with a potato as Vice President for four years. Mike Pence thanks you for your service, Mr. Quayle. Lest you think Quayle's ineptitude was a mere blip in the Bush legacy, he also appointed Clarence Thomas to the Supreme Court.

But it was Reagan, with his convenient and frequent lapses of memory, who had paved the way for people in power not to know what they were talking about or what was going on. No longer did the country require the best and brightest; it would be just fine with the Beverly Hillbillies teaming up with Beavis and Butthead in charge. Why would they risk looking like idiots? Because that feeds Reagan's narrative that the government is incompetent and in its place, you should put your trust in private enterprise, which by the way, has proven to be infinitely more incompetent but at least someone is making a billion dollars while doing it.

Then there was the clean-up of Iran-Contra. In all, dozens of people were indicted for their participation, eleven were convicted yet all were either vacated on appeal or pardoned. Those included among the pardons were the former Secretary of Defense, the Assistant Secretary of State, and a National Security Advisor. The one guy who didn't get a pardon was General Manuel Noriega, the authoritarian President of Panama, who had made the entire operation possible by allowing the unfettered passage of drug shipments through his country. When he threatened to go public with incriminating details about the operation that implicated Bush, the Marines were sent in to remove him from power. The reason cited for the invasion was that Noriega had been indicted on drug trafficking charges by grand juries in Miami and Tampa and that he had annulled Panama's election. It marked the first time in history that the US had invaded a sovereign country just to arrest one person. It also marked the first time in human history that the music of Rick Astley had been used as a weapon of war. Never Gonna Give You Up, indeed.

Before Bush was president, he was head of the CIA during Operation Condor. It was a program in which the US-backed repressive regimes and state-sponsored terrorism in South America that included the assassinations of opposition leaders. One of those assassinated was Orlando Letelier, a former subordinate to Chilean leader Salvador Allende and vocal critic of Augusto Pinochet. What made his assassination particularly notable is that it took place in Washington DC, and the car bomb that killed him also killed an American citizen. None of the people who organized or carried out the plot served more than six years in prison.

He was also the son of Prescott Bush and grandson of George Herbert Walker. That doesn't sound like such a big deal but both Prescott and George were part owners of the investment firm of W. A. Harriman, which later merged to become Brown Brothers Harriman and Co. And yes, they also participated in the Wall Street Putsch.

So George H.W. had ties to banking, but not just any bank. One of their clients was a man named Fritz Thyssen, the same Fritz Thyssen who was a German industrialist and primary financier of Adolf Hitler before he became Chancellor. Have you ever wondered why people in protests and campaigns almost always have uniform signs - printed in the same font and color – and there just happens to be a stage with microphones handy when the candidate stops by a park? It's men like Thyssen who make it happen and bankers like the Bushes who made Thyssen richer. Oh, and the funding for the original Harriman bank came from railroad money. That same railroad company was the one that built the railroad into Auschwitz.

I'm not saying that any of the Bush's were Nazis, even the ones who helped them make money. Every ultra-successful businessman will do business with the Devil himself if it means making good money. They'll hold their nose while shaking hands to sell their soul if the price is right. A perfect example is Fred Koch, father of the infamous Koch Brothers. He was a rabid anti-communist and one of the founders of the ultra-right-wing John Birch Society. That didn't stop him from selling his oil drill bit technology to the Soviets, and then helping them develop their vast oil resources. Another example is Alfred Sloan of General Motors, helping Adolf Hitler build not only the German economy but the German war machine as well. For their pre-war assistance, both Sloan and Henry Ford were awarded Germany's highest civilian honors. One of GM's shareholders brought the death camps to Sloan's attention in a letter written in 1943, asking whether or not GM should divest. In 1933, GM had bought 100% ownership of what was then Germany's largest auto manufacturer, Opel. During the war, they were actively producing blitz trucks for the Wehrmacht, as well as other machine parts for tanks and airplanes. They made blitzkrieg possible. They were also well aware of the slave labor being used to manufacture these things. But even death camps were not sufficient reason for Sloan. He replied that GM was not "in the business of politics", and that "in Germany, [GM] was a German company." The kicker is that both he and Henry Ford sued the US government for war reparations after World War 2 because their German factories had been bombed. They won a settlement of $44 million (equivalent to about $764 million today).

There is no mystery how the German economy after World War 1 transformed from being wracked by runaway inflation into the most dynamic economy in Europe. It wasn't solely due to the investment of two US auto companies and some magic dust from the Nazi economy fairy. Numerous American companies like IBM, ALCOA, CocaCola, Random House, DuPont, Eastman Kodak, Associated Press, Chase Manhattan Bank, Dow Chemical, Woolworth's, and General Electric were but the biggest names who were deeply vested in the rebirth of the German economy under Hitler. He gave them favorable terms and they made lots of money.

We see these kinds of interactions all the time with bankers laundering money for drug cartels. In 2020 it was revealed that banking giant HSBC had laundered billions for the Mexican drug cartels. Nor it is uncommon for billionaires to do business with murderous dictators. Both Donald Trump and Elon Musk have had very public business transactions with the Saudis and Vladimir Putin. So it is altogether expected that the Bush family, while they might not have shared ideology with Nazis, had no qualms about taking a percentage of the profits made from doing business with them.

This is what Lincoln was warning us about. And when Reagan made his speeches about a smaller government and wanting to privatize services the government had provided, these were the very people that he wanted to replace the government with.

Ancient DNA reveals fate of the mysterious Canaanites
https://www.science.org/content/article/ancient-dna-reveals-fate-mysterious-canaanites

How the Canaanites, Biblical frenemies of the Israelites, kept genetic integrity
https://www.timesofisrael.com/study-shows-canaanites-israelites-biblical-frenemies-kept-genetic-integrity/

DNA from the Bible's Canaanites lives on in modern Arabs and Jews
https://www.nationalgeographic.co.uk/history-and-civilisation/2020/05/dna-from-the-bibles-canaanites-lives-on-in-modern-arabs-and-jews

Military budget of the United States
https://en.wikipedia.org/wiki/Military_budget_of_the_United_States

U.S. Military Spending/Defense Budget 1960-2024
https://www.macrotrends.net/countries/USA/united-states/military-spending-defense-budget

The Problems With NAFTA
https://www.thebalancemoney.com/disadvantages-of-nafta-3306273

The business of making the trains to Auschwitz run on time
https://www.sfgate.com/opinion/article/The-business-of-making-the-trains-to-Auschwitz-2821685.php

Operation Condor
https://en.wikipedia.org/wiki/Operation_Condor

How Bush's grandfather helped Hitler's rise to power
https://www.theguardian.com/world/2004/sep/25/usa.secondworldwar?all=true

10 Famous Companies That Collaborated With Nazi Germany
https://historycollection.com/10-famous-companies-collaborated-nazi-germany/

10 US Companies That Worked with Nazi Germany
https://www.historydefined.net/us-companies-that-worked-with-nazi-germany/

Nazi documents reveal that Ford had links to Auschwitz
https://www.theguardian.com/world/1999/aug/20/julianborger1

Internal Combustion by Edwin Black
https://www.internalcombustionbook.com/

Nazi Nexus by Edwin Black
https://nazinexus.com/

Well-Intentioned Wolves

Moving on to one of the most polarizing presidents in recent memory... No, this is not about Obama. His legacy is largely middle-of-the-road borderline conservative, as we'll get to in a later chapter. The contentiousness that stemmed from his administration was almost entirely born from the fact that he was the first non-white president. There is an overwhelming amount of evidence to support that being a significant and deciding factor in the resistance against his policies.

But we're not talking about him yet. This chapter is about Bill Clinton, a polarizing president, and not for the reasons most think. Who cares if he got a blowjob from an intern?! It was certainly inappropriate, as was lying under oath in the deposition for the Paula Jones trial regarding sexual harassment. But that case was thrown out of court for lack of evidence. So in some ways, it is irrelevant what he said. And if every boss who ever got sexual favors from an underling were indicted for lying about it, there would be many more people in jail than there are now. Not saying that it's right by any stretch. Just saying it's not uncommon. Was he the first President to lie? Obviously not. Was he the first President to have an affair while in the White House? Don't make me laugh. There is credible evidence that at least ten Presidents had affairs while serving in the White House. Did this have any bearing on Clinton's policies? Did it affect his mental capacity to govern? Absolutely not. This should have been the stupidest, most ridiculous political scandal in US history. Unfortunately, it probably doesn't even rank in the top 25.

Clinton turned out to be Reagan's idea of a perfect Democrat: one who agreed with everything he said, but was on the other side of the aisle so that it looked like people had a choice. Like Reagan, Clinton waded knee-deep into welfare reform because poor people were seen as a big problem. He also passed sweeping crime laws that disproportionately affected the poor and began the militarization of police forces. The private prison industry exploded under Clinton. The number of people incarcerated more than tripled, from roughly 500,000 in 1989 to nearly 2 million by the time he left office. The US has 4% of the world's population, yet 16% of the world's incarcerated. The prison population did get as high as 2.3 million in 2008 but that's for the guy in the next chapter.

Clinton will be remembered as the president of failed compromises. He tried to negotiate with the hard-line conservatives (a lesson Obama should have learned from during his two terms) and ended up with a shit sandwich. He tried to pass comprehensive healthcare but ended up with nothing because the Republicans in Congress managed to convince voters that not only wasn't it in their best interest, but that the government would screw it up if it ever came to pass, echoing the Reagan mantra. Did they miss the part about the government being responsible for putting a man on the moon and providing people the electronic infrastructure to send silly memes and naked pictures to all their friends and co-workers via email and instant messages? Did they miss the part where the government delivers their regular mail to any address in the world for one-tenth the cost of the commercial overnight carriers? Evidently, the answer was yes because the Republicans took the House and made Newt Gingrich their speaker, who was and is perhaps the biggest bag of foul wind in US Congressional history.

Gingrich was responsible for ousting a Democratic Speaker for using a book deal to circumvent campaign finance laws while he himself was circumventing campaign finance laws with a book deal. He raised a stink about Democrats abusing the House banking rules which allowed them to carry overdrafts, while he himself had twenty-two overdrafts totaling thousands of dollars including one to the IRS for more than $9000. He led the charge for impeachment against Clinton for his affair with intern

Monica Lewinsky while he himself was carrying on an affair with one of his staffers who would become his third wife. He served divorce papers to his first wife while she was hospitalized with ovarian cancer in 1980 (the year after he was elected to Congress) so he could marry the woman who would become his second wife. Gingrich was quoted saying of his first wife, "She's not young enough or pretty enough to be the wife of the President. And besides, she has cancer." After the divorce, she had to raise money from her church congregation because Gingrich only paid $400 of support per month for her and their three children. In 1980, the salary of a congressman was $60,652.50 per year (which converts to nearly $250,000 in today's dollars). Even after a court ordered him to pay more, he refused to do so, citing his dry cleaning bills as a prohibitive expense. If there has ever been a more loathsome worm who projected onto others every sin and wrongdoing that he himself was committing than Newt Gingrich, there is no official record of him. He blamed his infidelities on his love for this country, all the while promoting Christian Nationalist politics. Evidently, he was unfamiliar with the separation of church and state clause in the First Amendment. Some might suggest that I should just go the full distance and call him a "pile of shit", but shit has substance; Gingrich never did. Eventually, though, his dirty deeds caught up to him and he was forced to resign by his own party after they lost seats in a mid-term election. He left with a record eighty-four ethics charges, although only one of them stuck meriting an official reprimand. He had claimed tax-exempt status for a college course run for political purposes. It was the first time ever that a Speaker had been reprimanded. The cost was essentially a $300,000 fine to reimburse the investigation expenses. That's quite the cleaning bill. The only reason I detail or even mention Gingrich is that much of his political playbook will be embraced and elaborated on by a future president: Donald Trump.

    One of Gingrich's most lasting impacts was the way he wrested away control in committees from the committee structure toward party leadership, particularly in the Appropriations

Committee. He instituted term limits for committee chairmen and changed the internal caucus rules so that they aligned more toward what party leadership wanted. So instead of members being ranked in the committees by their experience and tenure, it became strictly a popularity contest for the party leaders, in which they could remake the membership any way they saw politically expedient. The very composition of the committees became a political football. That's how Jim Jordan ended up on the judiciary committee and Marjorie Taylor Greene ends up on, well, any committee. So not only did they evolve toward hyper-partisanship, but it led to skyrocketing campaign contributions from lobbyists who could help shape them from the outside. Before Gingrich, committee membership was more stable, so the lobbyist knew what kind of legislation could and couldn't be passed because each member had a well-known history. After Gingrich, they could influence who was actually on the committee by simply donating more money to the leaders, thus stacking it with members who would certainly see things their way. That's one reason why the Citizens United decision was a godsend to them.

  Returning to Clinton, he did succeed in removing the protections of the Glass-Steagall Act, which was Depression Era legislation that separated commercial from investment banks. So even if a bank, like Citibank, had an investment arm, like Salomon Smith Barney, they could not use your deposits in their banks to invest in the stock market. He thought that removing that barrier would free up the banking industry to do anything it wanted, resulting in a booming economy. It worked for a while, but fast growth and growth for its own sake is not often a good thing, especially in an economy as titanic as that of the US. Unleashing the banks allowed them to start doing irresponsible things like investing in increasingly unstable commodities like mortgage-backed securities filled with subprime variable rate loans. Hello, 2007-2008 meltdown! Nobel-winning economist Joseph Stiglitz famously pointed out that if a bank is safely earning 2-3% by lending money for mortgages and such, but has a chance to earn ten times that in the stock market, where do you think they're gonna put your money? Without Clinton first unlocking the gates, Bush could never have opened them all the way, just like Reagan did with many of Carter's deregulation policies. Only Carter's were necessary for technology to grow; Clinton's were expedient for political donations to grow.

There were also a massive number of hostile takeovers and mergers during this period, which he also failed to regulate under anti-trust laws. Reagan had opened the door with his nearly non-existent enforcement of anti-trust laws, allowing more than 25,000 deals totaling more than $2 trillion in value during his eight-year presidency. Clinton upped the ante, standing by and allowing the creation of too-big-to-fail companies and the complete cannibalism of the media. Nine of the ten largest corporate mergers in history occurred between 1998 and 2000. *All* of them could have been stopped using existing anti-trust regulations. The volume of mergers increased ten-fold from 1992 to 2000, with more than $3 trillion worth of capital changing hands through mergers during that final year alone. Tech companies, many still in their infancy, were especially susceptible to these takeovers and the rapid consolidation left the economy ripe for a meltdown, which happened in late 2000 with the tech bubble bursting. Clinton had done nothing to regulate that industry which in the end, as it always does with unregulated capitalism, resulted in collapse.

In addition to the Great Depression, there had been collapses in 1837, 1857, 1873 (with over-speculation in railroads), 1890 (with banking over-speculation in foreign markets) which led to another in 1893 under the same auspices, and in 1907 (with over-speculation in the copper industry). The latter could have been potentially as disastrous as the Great Depression had mega-financier J.P. Morgan not pledged his own money to help the banking system remain solvent. This crisis led to the creation of the Federal Reserve System. Despite many lessons from history, Clinton did nothing to steer the industry, and with it, the economy, away from a meltdown.

The result of that merger-mania is that today we have four corporations that control 90% of *all* media – television, radio, movies, publishing – and a good portion of the remaining media are controlled by two right-wing megalomaniacs who literally want to fight each other on pay per view. Four banks own roughly 41% of all assets – savings, mortgages, loans - covered under the FDIC. Two companies control 80% of the telecom industry. Four control 70% of the airlines. Roughly 80% of all food produced and sold in this country comes from four companies. Walmart alone accounts for one in four dollars that Americans spend on groceries and captures more than half of grocery sales in forty-three metropolitan areas. Worse still, the largest shareholder in 88% of the companies on the S&P 500 is one of three investment firms: Blackrock, Vanguard, or State Street. Together they manage more than $11 trillion in assets, an amount that is greater than half of the GDP of the United States. Their only objective is to get the greatest return on shareholder investment.

One of the biggest problems with the baby boomer generation of Democrats, which includes Clinton and Obama, is that they have consistently tried to be Republican-lite when it came to business protections and regulations. The Democratic party's greatest strength since FDR was protecting the poor and underprivileged against the privileged. That's one of the reasons it had been hard for them to win presidential elections: they were going against the moneyed interests. They could only run on principles which is hard to do when the opposition was marketing a brand of get-rich populism. The problem with the Democrats courting corporations and Wall Street is that the Republicans can always promise more. Cut your taxes? So what, the GOP will eliminate healthcare. Over the last two decades, it has been especially evident that the Republican party only cares about millionaires and billionaires. For them, it is a sin to share anything with or help anyone who makes less money than they do. Since Congressmen make $174,000 a year, that works out to about 90% of the population.

Another similarity between Clinton and Reagan is their treatment of gay people. Reagan dismissed AIDS as a gay disease and repeatedly denied funding for research. Clinton simply wanted people to stop talking about gay people with his "Don't ask, Don't tell" policy in the military and the Defense of Marriage Act. The latter denied many of the rights of same-sex couples that were afforded to male-female couples. Both Reagan and Clinton stuck their fingers in their ears and shouted "I can't hear you" when it came to the many challenges facing that demographic.

His foreign policy legacy is no different when it came to short-sighted compromises. Hailed at the time as being progressive, the 1994 Budapest Memorandum assured the Ukraine that in exchange for giving up nearly 1900 nuclear warheads, the US, the UK, and Russia would agree to respect their sovereignty. It's true, Boris Yeltsin was president of Russia at the time, and Putin was still just First Deputy Chairman of St. Petersburg, five years from becoming Russia's next president. But the assurances that were given were never guarantees of military aid. So basically, if Ukraine was ever invaded, the US and UK would only be obliged to think about helping them. Sure, it was a bad deal for them to agree to, but they needed good relations with the West and no one ever thought that an ex-KGB agent with a history of criminal behavior would ever become president of Russia. I mean what country would ever elect a president who had participated in illegal intelligence operations? Other than the US with the previous administration, of course. As a result, Putin had no fear of retaliation from the West when he "annexed" Crimea in 2014, and then launched a full-scale invasion in 2022.

Just as Newt Gingrich had, Clinton opened the door for Donald Trump. Clinton "felt our pain" to appeal to a generation of blue-collar, salt-of-the-earth types who trusted that the government would help lift them. Trump would call these people "the poorly educated". Both Clinton and Trump betrayed that trust by giving away the barn and the keys to the treasury to the wealthy and corporate.

On the plus side, Clinton did recognize that Osama bin Laden was a real threat and on several occasions, the CIA taskforce he ordered to apprehend or kill him came very close to doing just that. There was a rumored cruise missile strike on the table in December of 1998 that might very well have killed him but it was decided jointly by both Clinton and his advisors that the collateral damage – 200 to 300 women and children plus the destruction of a good portion of the town of Kandahar – would have been too much to justify the action. The rest, as they say, is history. However, just to put things in perspective, after the first bombing of the World Trade Center, Clinton deemed that investigation a law enforcement matter and thus relaxed the laws that forbid the FBI and police from sharing information about the investigation with other agencies. His joint task force to find bin Laden didn't come into being until 1996, three years after the first attack. While it did net and convict the six people who carried out the bombing, it failed to trigger a larger investigation into the Al Queda network.

Some would say it's easy to criticize in retrospect because one never knows what will happen. That is true to a point. But there's also an equally valid point that most people are only afforded to look at things in retrospect because they don't have the real-time information the president has access to. So how many people would go ahead with a missile strike knowing that it would kill 300 innocents but also kill someone who, at that point, had already bombed two US embassies and the garage of the building in New York and would later bring down with passenger airliners filled with jet fuel? It seemed clear, even then, that death or incarceration were the only ways to stop bin Laden from carrying out more attacks and the former was far more likely than the latter. That proved true with the attacks on the USS Cole – which didn't have confirmation that Bin Laden was involved until Bush took office – and the 9/11 attack. Clinton passed on another missile strike in May of 1999 but decided not to because it was not clear that bin Laden was at the target location. That said, his administration was successful in thwarting a plot that would have detonated bombs in several locations around the world at various New Millennium celebrations. Still, what might have been.

Top Ten Presidents Who Had Affairs
https://www.thetoptens.com/leaders/presidents-who-had-affairs/

The True Extent of America's Food Monopolies
https://www.theguardian.com/environment/ng-interactive/2021/jul/14/food-monopoly-meals-profits-data-investigation

America's Monopoly Problem: Why It Matters and What We Can Do About It
https://ilsr.org/fighting-monopoly-power/americas-monopoly-problem-and-why-it-matters/

WAVE OF MERGERS, TAKEOVERS IS A PART OF REAGAN LEGACY
https://www.washingtonpost.com/archive/business/1988/10/30/wave-of-mergers-takeovers-is-a-part-of-reagan-legacy/e90598c2-628d-40fe-b9c6-a621e298671d/

The Man Who Broke Politics
https://www.theatlantic.com/magazine/archive/2018/11/newt-gingrich-says-youre-welcome/570832/

Newt Gingrich
https://en.wikipedia.org/wiki/Newt_Gingrich#cite_note-:10-9

Newt Gingrich's Legacy As A Political Commentator: Smears, Falsehoods, And Inflammatory Rhetoric
https://www.mediamatters.org/newt-gingrich/newt-gingrichs-legacy-political-commentator-smears-falsehoods-and-inflammatory

Glass–Steagall legislation
https://en.wikipedia.org/wiki/Glass%E2%80%93Steagall_legislation

Defense of Marriage Act
https://en.wikipedia.org/wiki/Defense_of_Marriage_Act

CFI's regularly published analyses of federal campaign finance
http://www.cfinst.org/data/historicalStats.aspx

How the 1994 Crime Bill Fed the Mass Incarceration Crisis
https://www.aclu.org/news/smart-justice/how-1994-crime-bill-fed-mass-incarceration-crisis

The Militarization of America's Police: A Brief History
https://fee.org/articles/the-militarization-of-americas-police-a-brief-history/

Clinton crime bill: Why is it so controversial?
https://www.bbc.com/news/world-us-canada-36020717

America's incarceration rate falls to lowest level since 1995
https://www.pewresearch.org/short-reads/2021/08/16/americas-incarceration-rate-lowest-since-1995/

Bush's Beans

If Clinton was bad, George W. Bush was by an order of magnitude worse. Any appraisal of the second Bush presidency must begin with his handling of Al Queda's terrorist attack that killed 2977 victims on September 11, 2001. More than 1400 rescue workers have subsequently died from exposure to the toxins present at Ground Zero in New York City. In addition, more than 1100 people who were working, living, or studying near the World Trade Center buildings have since been diagnosed with cancer-related to that exposure.

The 9/11 Commission investigating the attack reported that both Clinton and Bush had not been well-served by the FBI and the CIA. Perhaps there is some truth to that. Both agencies had pieces of the puzzle that could have led to the interdiction of the Al Queda participants and were either by law or out of distrust not sharing with each other. However, immediately after taking office Bush removed cabinet-level access that had been granted under Clinton to national security expert and counter-terrorism chief for the National Security Council Richard Clarke. He had been warning both administrations that bin Laden and Al Queda were serious threats. Where Clinton had listened, Bush had no interest in hearing what he had to say. In January of 2001, he had written a memo calling attention to the growing Al Queda threat. At a deputies meeting in April, he advised that the US put pressure against the Taliban and Al-Queda by arming the Northern Alliance in Afghanistan. He also advised that the US resume drone flights in hopes of targeting Al Queda. At a July gathering at the White House that included members of the FAA, the Coast Guard, the FBI, the Secret Service, and INS, he told them that Al Queda was planning "something really spectacular that was going to happen here, and it's going to happen soon." In

August of 2001, he handed the president a report outlining that they were planning an attack using airplanes. Bush and his advisors dismissed it all, despite these reports being about the same guy who had bombed the World Trade Center in 1993, blown up two US embassies in Kenya and Tanzania killing 224 and injuring at least 4000 people in 1998, and was the likely (later confirmed) author of the attack on the USS Cole in 2000. Given the repeated warnings and the capability of the threat, one would think a president would take executive action. Bush did nothing.

After the tragedy, he went into overdrive exploiting the righteous anger of the American citizenry. He authorized the torture of detainees (or what the administration labeled as "enhanced interrogation techniques" but everyone who has ever experienced them calls them torture), spying on the citizens of the United States with the Patriot Act (which Obama re-authorized until it expired in 2020), sent troops to Afghanistan and gave the go-ahead for the second invasion of Iraq under the pretense that somehow the 9/11 terrorists were being funded by Saddam Hussein. Fifteen of the 19 terrorists were in fact from Saudi Arabia, a Shia country primarily opposed to the brand of Islam (Sunni) commonly practiced in Iraq. Yet something had to be done to show the American people that they weren't just running around with their hands in the air.

General Wesley Clark, a distinguished and decorated officer who had served as the Supreme Allied Commander of NATO under Clinton, said this:

"About ten days after 9/11, I went through the Pentagon and I saw Secretary Rumsfeld and Deputy Secretary Wolfowitz. I went downstairs just to say hello to some of the people on the Joint Staff who used to work for me, and one of the generals called me in. He said, "Sir, you've got to come in and talk to me a second." I said, "Well, you're too busy." He said, "No, no." He says, "We've made the decision we're going to war with Iraq." This was on or about the 20th of September. I said, "We're going to war with Iraq? Why?" He said, "I don't know." He said, "I guess they don't know what else to do." So I said, "Well, did they find some information connecting Saddam to al-Qaeda?" He said, "No, no." He says, "There's nothing new that way. They just made the decision to go to war with Iraq." He said, "I guess it's like we don't know what to do about terrorists, but we've got a good military and we can take down governments." And he said, "I guess if the only tool you have is a hammer, every problem has to look like a nail." So I came back to see him a few weeks later, and by that time we were bombing in Afghanistan. I said, "Are we still going to war with Iraq?" And he said, "Oh, it's worse than that." He reached over on his desk. He picked up a piece of paper. And he said, "I just got this down from upstairs" -- meaning the Secretary of Defense's office -- "today." And he said, "This is a memo that describes how we're going to take out seven countries in five years, starting with Iraq, and then Syria, Lebanon, Libya, Somalia, Sudan and, finishing off, Iran." I said, "Is it classified?" He said, "Yes, sir." I said, "Well, don't show it to me."

    In 2003, when no link to Hussein could be established, they used the allegation that he was not allowing UN inspections of certain facilities rumored to be producing either chemical or biological weapons. When neither of those were found, the reason cited for the invasion was that Hussein had been trying to build the capability to make them. They would have found more evidence had they accused him of producing crystal meth. So in addition to the thousands of Americans who died as a result of the 9/11 attack, an additional 4,492 service members died serving in Iraq from 2003 to 2012, when they were finally withdrawn under Obama. In addition, more than 32,000 service members were wounded, and more than a quarter of the 1.5 million who served at least one tour there came home with some kind of physical or psychological disability. In total, more than $800 billion was spent on the endeavor, none of it funded by increased revenue, thus adding to the debt, including more than $9 billion in cash that was somehow misplaced on a tarmac in Baghdad and never recovered.

Bush quoted British General Stanley Maude trying to reassure concerned Iraqis by saying "We are coming as liberators" to free them from the tyrannical and homicidal rule of Saddam Hussein. However, it was under British rule and colonial exploitation that precipitated nearly fifty years of political unrest and a string of military coups that ultimately resulted in Hussein seizing power in the first place. Needless to say, they were not reassured. In fact, one Iraqi journalist, Muntadahr al-Zaidi threw both of his shoes at Bush during a press conference in protest. The numbers told the true story: a survey conducted by Lancet, one of the world's most respected medical journals, concluded that 601,027 Iraqis died violent deaths as a direct result of that invasion. Other estimates go as high as a million. Numerous war crimes were also committed including the violations of detainees at Abu Ghraib prison, the Nisour Square and Haditha massacres, the Hamdania incident, and the Mahmudiyah rape and killings.

To add insult to injury, by the time Bush left office in 2009, the administration had stopped looking for bin Laden because they said he wasn't as important as trying to dismantle Al Queda. But that begs the question: doesn't killing or capturing the leader of a terrorist group expedite dismantling the organization that looks to him for guidance? And who was to say that he wasn't planning to attempt another attack, this time using fissile materials? He had already tried to buy uranium as early as 1993. Money would not have been a problem. He was the son of a Saudi billionaire air-conditioning magnate and had more than enough money at his disposal to acquire the necessary materials. He only needed a willing and discreet seller, and the world after the fall of the USSR had plenty of them. We simply were extremely lucky that the people who illegally sell weapons had enough integrity to believe that bin Laden was too crazy even for them to arm with something truly dangerous.

In addition to the incompetent 9/11 response and the disastrous decision to invade Iraq, and then occupy it for a decade, the Bush administration also managed to put us at greater threat of nuclear annihilation by withdrawing from the ABM treaty with Russia/Soviet Union (which by Bush's terms in office was under Vladimir Putin). He also did nothing to address global climate change rejecting the Kyoto Protocol, a worldwide agreement to reduce greenhouse gas emissions, because it would create economic setbacks for the US and didn't place the same restrictions on emerging third-world countries. He appointed John Bolton, an outspoken critic of the UN who had called for its abolition, to be the US ambassador to it. In short, Bush put a big mustachioed frowny face on the middle finger he gave to the rest of the world.

If that wasn't catastrophic enough, Bush was a complete disaster on domestic issues as well. His administration's incompetent response to the 2005 Hurricane Katrina disaster left nearly 2000 people dead and tens of thousands stranded and/or homeless. It took the National Guard three days to finally get fresh water to the victims in the city, and another forty days to get the last of the flood water pumped out of the city. The final damage was estimated to be more than $100 billion.

He authorized a spending bill that included subsidizing the cost of Viagra by Medicaid, yet underfunded No Child Left Behind by $800 million. He vetoed federal funding for stem cell research. He gutted the Clean Water Act by carving out a loophole allowing coal and other mining companies to dump their waste into waterways and groundwater. This paved the way for the fracking boom that began in the middle of the decade, peaked around 2012, and then slowly declined as people realized their groundwater was not only poisoned by fracking chemicals but also flammable. Who needs a dracarys or a B-52 when you can use tap water?

When he didn't like a law that prohibited him from doing something, he simply issued signing statements. These had been simply presidential comments on laws that had passed. There are two types: the first is essentially a 'thanks' or praise for what a bill does. The second, and this is what Bush was notable for, was a legal argument that either claimed that a particular portion of the bill was unconstitutional, or that it didn't apply to the president and therefore he didn't have to abide by it.

The first president to use them was James Monroe. Until Reagan came into office thirty-four presidents later, they were a relatively rare occurrence, with only seventy-five ever submitted that challenged the constitutional limits of the executive office. Reagan issued 250 statements in all, of which eighty-six (or more than all previous presidents combined) contained some challenge to the law. George H. W. Bush used 228, of which one hundred-seven contained some legal challenge. Clinton set the record with 381 signing statements but only seventy raised a constitutional objection. Bush issued a mere 161 statements but they contained more than 1,200 constitutional challenges, which was twice as many as all previous presidents combined. The man who had rationalized that they should be used by the president as a legislative weapon like a line-item veto was a staff attorney for the Justice Department Office of Legal Counsel under Reagan named Samuel Alito. He became a Supreme Court Justice under George W. Bush. Extending the Bush connection to the present, among the members of the legal team that engineered his 2000 election win in the "hanging chad" controversy during the Florida vote count, were current Chief Justice John Roberts (whom Bush appointed) and Trump-appointed Associate Justices Brett Kavanaugh and Amy Coney Barrett. Nice work if you can get it, eh?

If this were any other president, Bush's ties to both the Enron scandal (Enron CEO Kenneth Lay had long been a friend of the Bush's and was one of his biggest financial supporters, committed fraud on a massive scale, leaving millions of people without power and the Arthur Anderson accountancy, one of the five largest in the world, out of business and criminally indicted) and the Jack Abramoff scandal (Abramoff was a GOP lobbyist with close ties to Bush Chief of Staff Karl Rove and had on numerous occasions brokered meetings with Bush for political leaders around the world, but was convicted of wire fraud, bribery, tax evasion, and conspiracy to defraud four Native American tribes for lobbying fees) would take up more than a paragraph. But those pale by comparison to the big one.

Between 2000 and 2007, the US accounted for more than a third of the global consumption of securities. Under Clinton, investment firms had been granted the ability to use commercial bank funds (your deposits, your 401k funds, etc.) to speculate in the stock market. One of the more popular instruments was a bundle of mortgages wrapped into one security called a mortgage-backed security. As long as people paid their mortgages, it was a pretty safe investment. However, under Reagan, banks started becoming publicly traded corporations, thereby transferring the risk of lending from the private partnership that owned the bank to public shareholders, who demanded a return on their investment. This incentivizes the banks to assume more risk to ensure the necessary returns. At first, only government-sponsored lenders like Fannie Mae (the Federal National Mortgage Association) and Ginnie Mae (Government National Mortgage Association) could create these mortgage securities, but Reagan began allowing public companies like Salomon Brothers to do so as well under the Secondary Market Enhancement Act. The Tax Reform Act of 1986 further offered incentives for people to get mortgages by making the interest paid on them tax deductible. The Equal Credit Opportunity Act of 1974 had made it illegal to discriminate against giving mortgage loans to people based on anything but their credit, so the only question was how to get more people to buy houses. Clinton authored a National Homeownership Strategy that set minimum FICO scores for people to qualify for mortgage loans, but subprime lenders (banks that charge higher rates due to the risk involved with lending to a low credit score buyer) found ways to get around the standard by offering gimmicky loans like balloon rate loans, which start low at first so that the buyer can increase their credit score but later escalate to much higher than normal interest rates. In 1990, JP Morgan invented an investment instrument called a credit default swap, which is a bet that the targeted asset (like a stock or a fund) will default on its financial obligation. Beginning under Clinton but continuing under Bush, the Federal Reserve decreased the interest rate for lending from 6.5% in May 2000 down to 1.75% by December 2001, down further to 1% by 2003, all to get more people buying houses. In addition, Bush passed the Economic Growth and Tax Relief Reconciliation Act of 2001 and the Jobs and Growth Tax Relief Reconciliation Act of 2003, both of which were huge giveaways to the rich costing the government trillions in revenue. They reduced the top rate by nearly 5% as well as lowered rates on capital gains. They also increased benefits for contributions to tax shelters and eliminated the estate tax. This meant the wealthy had much more money to invest. So they did. By 2006, nearly 30% of the real estate market was comprised of investment property and more than $600 billion had been invested in subprime mortgages. The mortgage denial rate had dropped from 29% under Clinton down to 14%. With the availability of credit default swaps, people started betting on where the failures might happen. Then people started betting that the credit default swaps would they themselves fail. And so on. The inevitable defaults did start to happen in 2007, and by the time the carnage ended in 2008, the Treasury Department estimated that more than $19.2 trillion of the US economy had been lost. That's the conservative estimate. The average American household lost a third of their worth, but that hides the fact that the bottom 25% of income earners lost more than 60% of their net worth. The ones at the top, the top 5%, were shielded by bailouts. They lost just 13%. Millions lost jobs, homes, and retirement savings. It was estimated that in 2010, 46.2 million Americans were living in poverty, which was the highest number in the 50+ years that the government had been keeping track of the statistic. So in addition to his other disasters, George W. Bush abetted and presided over the worst financial disaster since the Great Depression.

  If you're scoring at home, before Reagan there were no depressions or financial meltdowns over the previous 50 years since the New Deal, breaking the cycle of economic crashes every

15-20 years that had plagued the US economy since the 1830s. From 1981 to 2008, beginning with Reagan and his "business first and always" politics, there were six: the 1980-1983 Recession, Black Monday in 1987, the Savings and Loan Crisis in 1986, the 1992 Recession, the Dot Com bubble in 2000-2002, and the 2007-2008 meltdown. Three Republican presidents and one Democrat who acted like a Republican.

So was everything bad under Bush? Obviously not. He initiated the "No Child Left Behind" program aimed at improving elementary and secondary education. Of course, he underfunded the program forcing the state governments to make up the rest of the funding, which was not problematic for states that generate much of the federal revenue (primarily "blue" or democratically-run states) but was quite burdensome for "red" Republican-run states that had large low-income populations. The program standardized teaching, which sounded like a great idea but in practice led to teachers structuring their classes to pass standardized tests rather than teaching the subject matter. The tax reforms also limited how much teachers could deduct for teaching aids and supplies that would bring creativity into the environment, further neutering the instruction. The long-term downside was that rather than teaching students to think it focused on rewarding them for absorbing data. Thus spawned an entire generation of social media personalities who focus on one aspect of an issue to gain attention rather than understanding it as a whole. But at least he tried to do the right thing, right?

Another effort that turned out much better was his campaign to fight the global AIDS pandemic, PEPFAR (The President's Emergency Plan for AIDS Relief). The US had been spending about $500 million worldwide per year on AIDS relief. PEPFAR committed $20 billion and recruited resources from the Departments of State, Defense, Health and Human Services, Commerce and Labor as well as the Centers for Disease Control (CDC) and the Peace Corps in a coordinated strategy of prevention and education, treatment and care for patients and their communities. It is estimated that the program saved 25 million lives and stemmed the spread of the disease primarily in Africa through anti-viral treatments, testing, counseling, and financial support for millions of children orphaned by the disease.

In 2008, the History News Network conducted an unscientific poll among 109 professional historians. That poll found that among those asked, 98% believed that the George W. Bush presidency was a failure and 61% believed it to be the worst in history. After reading that, the leadership of the GOP reportedly said, "Hold my beer." Jokes aside, what is important to remember is that even the worst president has the capacity to inspire hope, even if the only people they provide it to are on another continent.

9/11 Commission Report
https://en.wikipedia.org/wiki/9/11_Commission_Report

Richard Clarke
https://en.wikipedia.org/wiki/Richard_A._Clarke

Dramatic new details released of Bush, Cheney dealing with 9/11 attacks
https://abcnews.go.com/Politics/dramatic-details-released-bush-cheney-dealing-911-attacks/story?id=93083567

Getting Away with Torture: The Bush Administration and Mistreatment of Detainees
https://www.hrw.org/report/2011/07/12/getting-away-torture/bush-administration-and-mistreatment-detainees

Iraq by the Numbers
https://www.dpc.senate.gov/docs/fs-112-1-36.pdf

U.S. Says Bin Laden Aide Tried to Get Nuclear Materia
https://www.nytimes.com/1998/09/26/world/us-says-bin-laden-aide-tried-to-get-nuclear-material.html

Why did help take so long to arrive?
https://www.theguardian.com/world/2005/sep/03/hurricanekatrina.usa1

Hurricane Katrina
https://www.britannica.com/event/Hurricane-Katrina

Bush Administration Approves Most Damaging Change to Clean Water Act in Decades
https://earthjustice.org/press/2002/bush-administration-approves-most-damaging-change-to-clean-water-act-in-decades

The fracking boom is over. Where did all the jobs go?
https://www.technologyreview.com/2021/07/01/1027822/fracking-boom-jobs-industry/

Presidential Signing Statements:Constitutional and Institutional Implications
https://sgp.fas.org/crs/natsec/RL33667.pdf

Enron's Close Ties to Bush
https://abcnews.go.com/Politics/story?id=121269&page=1

Did Abramoff have close ties to White House?
https://www.nbcnews.com/id/wbna11460885

Abramoff Bragged of Ties to Rove
https://www.latimes.com/archives/la-xpm-2006-feb-15-na-abramoff15-story.html

GOP Chief, Abramoff Linked In New Government Report
https://forward.com/news/391/gop-chief-abramoff-linked-in-new-government-repor/

2008 Financial Crisis Cost Americans $12.8 Trillion: Report
https://finance.yahoo.com/blogs/daily-ticker/2008-financial-crisis-cost-americans-12-8-trillion-145432501.html

The Average American Household Lost a Third of Its Net Worth During the Recession
https://www.smithsonianmag.com/smart-news/average-american-household-lost-third-their-net-worth-during-recession-180952191/

How Much Did the Financial Crisis Cost?
https://www.pbs.org/wgbh/frontline/article/how-much-did-the-financial-crisis-cost/

The Bush Tax Cuts and Their Impact on the Economy
https://www.thebalancemoney.com/president-george-bush-tax-cuts-3306331

Results and Impact – PEPFAR
https://www.state.gov/results-and-impact-pepfar/

Obama

There's an argument to be made that had there never been a George W. Bush, there never would have been a Barack Obama. Voters were desperate for any sign of hope that the previous eight years were as bad as it could get. They wanted someone who promised something new. Obama was one of the few congressmen who had refused to endorse the war in Iraq and offered a message of change we could believe in. His campaign devoted considerable resources to social media and non-standard forms of getting the message out like a website to counter smears by his opposition. In many ways, he, not Bush, was the first 21st-century President.

OK, so let's start with the obviously good: Civil Rights. There is no question that Obama had a huge positive impact on many civil rights in this country. He signed laws that gave women a legal recourse in cases of wage discrimination and opened up many freedoms to homosexuals that heterosexuals take for granted (ability to serve in the military, marriage, etc.). That said, Obama had not been a vocal advocate for gay marriage until his vice president, Joe Biden, replied in an interview that "of course gay marriage should be legal". It wasn't until after the immediate groundswell of support for Biden's statement that Obama got on board. So in that regard, he was an opportunist. However, it is always better to be on the right side of history when you're an opportunist, than the wrong one, and he was definitely on the right side. He rightly gets credit for naming a cabinet that gave women more positions of power than any previously and was the most ethnically and orientatively diverse. That might not seem like a big deal to many, but to those seeking role models who represent their background, it is as Biden later opined "a very big deal". Another area that was almost entirely good was his modification of how drug offenses were handled in the criminal justice system, giving courts sentencing options in cases of non-violent first-time offenders serving their time in drug rehab programs. That's a much more constructive response than sentencing them to mandatory time in prison.

He was reasonably active on the environment, putting limits on offshore drilling, protecting many lands that were either sacred to Native Americans or important habitats for native species, and addressing climate change with actual policy instead of just lip service by signing onto the Paris Agreement. The latter was not scientifically a monumental step to take because the accord does way too little to fix the problem but the truth about international treaties is that they rarely enact seismic change from the start. For example, to get to the point where we are concerning nuclear disarmament with the Soviet Union/Russia, the two countries have negotiated and signed eight treaties (SALT I & II, START, SORT, New START, INF, ABM, and NPT), each one addressing another aspect of disarmament. The act of getting 196 countries to agree on anything and then signing onto it was the important part.

The next group of accomplishments has both good and bad sides. For example, in the fight against global terrorism, Obama deservedly gets credit for the death of Osama bin Laden, especially after the Bush administration gave up looking for him. Even if you make the argument that bin Laden wasn't tactically important to the upcoming plans of Al Queda, he was an important symbol for the violently anti-American sentiment around the world because he had successfully attacked America and suffered few if any consequences up until that fateful night. Obama understood this and changed that perception. Conversely, Obama should certainly not be faulted for the rise of ISIL. The fact that most of ISIL's leadership was comprised of disenfranchised Iraqis should give a strong clue as to who is truly responsible. The Bush administration had essentially fired everyone in the Iraqi army after the successful overthrow of

Saddam Hussein but then chose not to disarm them. For all intents and purposes, he fired them from their jobs but let them keep the guns. A wiser choice would have been to give them new jobs of policing the new Iraq and keeping the peace during what turned out to be an extremely expensive occupation rather than trying to train an entire country's police force from scratch. So, no, ISIL is not on Obama.

However, drone strikes around the world to kill suspected terrorists could probably qualify as war crimes or at the very least, assassinations. Not only are they only "suspected" terrorists but often innocents are killed when a missile or a bomb hits their houses. They're not all bin Laden. People in the countries that are targeted for these strikes develop a sense of hopelessness, that no rule of law protects them from extrajudicial killings. That powerlessness drives the survivors to resort to terrorism. Adding to this promotional video is that Obama did little or nothing to prosecute those responsible for war crimes that occurred under the previous administration. Perhaps that was too much of a gray area for his advisors to demand tribunals, but people in many other countries did not see it that way.

Some will fault him for not doing enough in reaction to the annexation of Crimea in 2014, which further emboldened Putin to invade Ukraine in 2022. However, at the time, much of Europe held isolationist views and was unwilling to help even with the sanctions that were ultimately placed. In addition, the government in Ukraine still had many members with Soviet sympathies. Victor Yanukovich, the Ukrainian president who was removed from power in early 2014 by their parliament was, for all intents and purposes, a Russian puppet. When the warrant was issued for his arrest over the deaths of more than 100 protesters, he fled to Russia. He was convicted and sentenced in absentia for high treason. A more substantial US involvement in that moment might have only triggered a wider escalation of civil unrest and given Putin more pretense to escalate his annexation to a full-on invasion. It was Obama's successor who supported the annexation, undermined Ukrainian policy and its leaders as well as questioned the alliance between the US and Ukraine, thereby giving Putin the opening he sought for a second shot at taking the country.

As for national security, Obama did nothing to reign in the invasiveness of the Patriot Act until a CIA computer intelligence analyst named Edward Snowden leaked to the press about illegal spying programs targeting all Americans. Hackers had grown increasingly sophisticated in their ability to attack the national security apparatus and with access to sensitive and information warehouses, the kind of data harvesting sanctioned under the Patriot Act made Americans less safe, not more. Regarding Snowden and other whistleblowers, Obama was no friend, with eight prosecutions under the Espionage Act, more than double all previous presidents combined, including jail time for the guy who leaked the information about CIA torture under Bush. Yet none of the people who authorized the torture were ever criminally tried or punished. Only the grunts who carried out the orders served time. There was also no jail time or even an indictment for General David Patreus who leaked classified information to his journalist mistress, Paula Broadwell. Obama just quietly accepted his resignation. Although the Republicans in Congress posed a significant obstacle to him closing Guantanamo, he nevertheless didn't seem to protest too much that he had someplace to offshore those he didn't want protected by the Constitution. The problem with this measured approach to what are clear violations of the 4th and 14th Amendments in the name of national security is that there is always the possibility, God forbid, that voters might be persuaded to elect a know-nothing asshat with visions of vindictive authoritarianism as a president, who might be tempted to abuse that tenuously gained power. The first rule of law in making any law is to try to make it as idiot-proof as possible because one never knows when a rabid orangutan is gonna be in charge and try to find ways to abuse it.

As for the economy under Obama, he was essentially given the remnants of Dresden in the aftermath of World War 2 and told to "rebuild it in four years" (note: the actual Dresden is still being rebuilt more than 70 years later). The national debt skyrocketed under Obama but that was largely due to the debt engine created by his predecessor. To combat it he signed a bailout package of similar size to the one Bush signed (albeit with a few more strings that made sure that bankers just didn't pocket the money as they had with the first one). He then pushed the Federal Reserve to start buying some of the toxic assets and infuse the economy with cash so that the markets wouldn't completely collapse (the official term was "qualitative easing"). Over the next five years, the Fed would take on $4.5 trillion in bad debt. The policy worked in the short term as by the end of his second term, the economy had largely stabilized and was growing at a strong steady pace. Long term, however, it would be a driving factor in the growing concerns over inflation.

Detractors noted that the GDP was flat under Obama, apparently forgetting that he had successfully navigated a worldwide financial meltdown. They said he was the first two-term president since they've been measuring to not have 3% growth in any year. What they conveniently forget is that government spending is in the calculation of GDP and includes servicing the interest on the debt which had exploded because the government was covering so much of the bad debt that had been run up by Wall Street. Obama was forced to reduce spending to get the debt under control. When I say 'forced', I do mean to use that specific term because in 2011 he and the Republican Congress passed a law called the Budget Control Act that stated if they could not agree on how the budget needed to be reduced, that automatic draconian cuts in government spending would be enacted. Since the Republican Congress had stated early on that they had no intention of helping an Obama presidency, they did not reach a consensus. The Sequestration, as it was called, went into effect and billions were cut from government spending, which made the interest payments on the debt even more consuming. The irony is that the Republican Congress largely ignored the spending freeze over the next decade and many of the cuts targeting military spending came in areas that were already being phased out. Still, it should be noted that the US economy recovered faster historically than average ones do after such a setback, and it grew faster than those in the European Union.

That said, one has to look at where that growth occurred. Economists are all about efficiency so when they are talking about measures like GDP increasing, they don't really care who is being affected. As former Clinton Secretary of Labor Robert Reich succinctly put it:

"They typically define an "efficient" policy as one where people who benefit from it could compensate the losers and still come out ahead. But this way of looking at things leaves out three big realities:

(1) In a society of widening inequality, the winners are often wealthier than the losers. So even if they fully compensate the losers, those losers may feel even less well off relative to the wealthy winners.

(2) As a practical matter, the winners almost never compensate the losers. Most of the losers from trade – the millions whose good jobs have been lost – don't even have access to unemployment insurance. And "trade adjustment assistance" is a joke.

(3) Finally, those whose paychecks have been declining because of trade don't make up for those declines through access to cheaper goods and services from abroad. Yes, the cheaper goods help. But adjusted for inflation, their hourly pay is still lower than it used to be."

So while the economy certainly wasn't as bad as Republicans made it out to be with their nonsense about the GDP and the debt they ran up, neither was it as good as the Democrats made it sound when they talked about how great the stock market was doing because the vast majority of Americans couldn't participate in it to a point where it would make a significant contribution to their lives. That still hasn't substantially changed for the majority of Americans. It hardly matters if unemployment figures have improved when most of the new employment is coming from minimum-wage jobs.

Obama's regulation of Wall Street after the crash was certainly measured. He can't be completely faulted for the limitations because of a historically obstructive Congress, but there's little question he would have had public support for prosecutions of the people responsible for the 2008 failure, namely the bankers who green-lighted every recklessly risky investment using other people's money. Instead, he invited people like Jamey Dimon of JP Morgan Chase and former Goldman Sachs CEO Hank Paulson (who was Treasury Secretary under Bush) to "advise" him on how they should be regulated. None were prosecuted for fraud despite the widespread evidence of it.

There were two important developments in his response to the meltdown: 1) the Federal Government gained greater oversight as to how much debt banks can handle as well as target them for extra regulation if a bank gets "too big to fail" and 2) the creation of the Consumer Financial Protection Bureau which has helped reign in some of the abuses in the credit card industry. However, as we've seen time and again, Presidents eventually leave office and their policies are then subject to the whims of their successors.

Despite the financial constraints of a crippled economy, Obama did manage to achieve what Clinton had not and passed some healthcare reform, which, and I'm not making this up, Republicans tried to repeal sixty-three times. The greater irony is that the reform he brought to Congress was the same one that Republican Robert Dole had campaigned with against Clinton, one that Republicans and twenty bi-partisan sponsors crafted for S.1770 in the 103rd Congress, and one very similar to one that had been enacted in Massachusetts by then-governor Mitt

Romney, also a Republican. The plan had been originally proposed by the Heritage Foundation, a conservative think tank that Reagan frequently cited. Yet they were voting against their own plan sixty-three times because it had been repurposed by Obama. It passed in late 2010 and the last vote to remove it was in 2016 (Obama's last full year in office) which means they averaged a vote to overturn the Affordable Care Act (ACA) once per month for five years. Granted, it would have been better for everyone (except the health insurance and pharmaceutical companies) had Obama been able to pass a comprehensive plan like those in Europe because the government could assure savings due to high volume, decreased administration costs, and no profit taking. But passing something that monumental against an openly hostile Congress might have taken decades to pass. It should be noted that as of 2019, the ACA had saved consumers an estimated $2.3 trillion in medical expenses that they would have incurred under the previous largely unregulated system.

That's not to say it doesn't still have problems in need of solving but almost all of them stem from a Supreme Court ruling which allowed Republican-governed states to refuse federal funding for the expansion of Medicaid, and insurance companies to pick and choose markets where they wanted to offer coverage. Why would they do that? Did I mention that Republicans voted to repeal it sixty-three times?

Obama did benefit from a drop in oil prices in part because OPEC and other oil producers began to see the writing on the wall: green energy was here to stay and they had to preserve their market share. Obama played a role in that energy revolution with a $3.4 billion investment in the power grid and another $80 billion investment in clean energy development. And before anyone goes off on what a disaster Solyndra (a solar panel company) was, and that Obama's green energy initiative was a failure, the Department of Energy subsidized/loaned money to more than 1300 companies under many different programs and fewer than 10% went bankrupt. Solyndra was one of five that failed in a group of more than sixty companies in one such program, which means the government had a success rate of more than 90% just in that group. Show me any venture capitalist who has that kind of success rate and I would urge you to give them everything you own to invest that isn't nailed down. Fund managers and speculators would kill to have such a success rate, especially in an emerging market. Even Bill Gates said that the federal government does a fantastic job of investing money. All total the number of failed companies lost about $780 million of that initial $80 billion (less than 1%), of which Solyndra lost a little more than $500 million. Balance that against some of the successes, like Tesla, which was loaned about $465 million. They paid back their loan early and it is now the largest automobile company in the world by market capitalization, worth about $650 *billion* as of April 2023. According to that measure, it's worth as much as the next eight companies on the list - Toyota, Porsche, BYD, Mercedes, Volkswagen, BMW, Stellantis (which owns Dodger and Chrysler) and Ford - combined. If you're scoring at home, GM is ranked 9th. Of course, that's just revealing what the market thinks Telsa will be worth. Right now, they rank 11th in overall annual revenue at $81 billion, which ain't half bad for a one-time half-billion-dollar investment. That one investment paid off more than the Obama administration loaned out.

By nearly any reasonable standard, that program has been wildly successful. If there's anything to complain about it's that Obama's green energy policy didn't do nearly enough. He could have made it the new space race, competing with China for market dominance in green energy. China has invested more than a trillion dollars in green energy technology, $546 billion in 2022 alone. They account for nearly half of the world's spending on renewable energy and spend four times what the US does developing it. That is where the future lies, not in trying to pump oil from beneath the tundra.

Another energy policy where Obama came up short was fossil fuels. Sure, he made BP pay $20 billion for the Deepwater

Horizon disaster, but he didn't make any improvements to the regulatory agency that handles offshore drilling so a similar disaster is inevitable. The wildlife and the industries associated with it like fishing still have not fully recovered. Oh, and BP got a $5 billion tax break out of the deal. He rejected the Keystone Pipeline but when it came to the Dakota Pipeline did practically nothing until it became clear that this might become a black mark on his legacy. It was then that he pushed the Army Corps of Engineers to deny the easement necessary for construction. I get that Big Oil has a stranglehold on the government's energy policy (although had Reagan continued Carter's path, things would probably have been very different) but as any self-defense expert will tell you, the key to breaking someone's stranglehold is not to let them keep strangling you.

Obama liked to say that he "didn't want the perfect to get in the way of the good", but that was just another way of saying that he was dealt a crappy hand due to big business misadventures. Rather than trying to enact sweeping reform, he had to accept help from those same big businesses to keep the ship afloat and restore some sense of normalcy. In theory, he could have taken the opportunity to implement a new paradigm, where the wealthy pay the tax rate they're rumored to have, and where corporations have to play on a level playing field with small business. Such a bold vision would have carried great risk. It could have shocked the system into a full-blown depression thus placing a stigma on any future non-white male presidential candidates by painting them as potentially too radical. However, the pay-off could have also been as seismic and as popular as the New Deal.

So while perfection is too much to ask of anyone and good is good enough most of the time, after the previous two decades, America needed better than good. They needed someone who actually delivered on the Hope and Change. What they got was a glimmer of it and then a lot more of the status quo: socialism for the wealthy, ruthless capitalism for everyone else. Not only that but they also got a touch of Big Brother/Soviet-style violation of privacy. As Ben Franklin famously said,

"Those who would give up essential Liberty to purchase a little temporary Safety, deserve neither Liberty nor Safety."

I get why the government spies on us because the most dangerous criminals and terrorists are as smart and ruthless as Genghis Khan. I also know that the feds could care less about 99.9999% of what you do or watch on the internet. The problem is that they can't secure any of that information. There is always some hacker, and now with AI becoming more sophisticated, more potential for data breaches where that information is compromised. The government shouldn't have it because no one should have it. It's not like the hackers are going to spend the time to hack a billion computers when they only need to hack one or two really big data centers. Again, the first rule of law is to make it idiot proof and if you can't do that, then that probably shouldn't be a law. Similarly, if you're going to make a policy, make sure that it is extremely difficult to abuse it or its product. As smart as Obama was as President, he didn't do that.

That said, he should be given the "Jackie Robinson exception" for at least part of his tenure. For the first couple of years of his career Robinson (as well as Larry Doby in the American League) was not allowed to fight back when injustices were committed against him on the field and his performance suffered. He was not allowed to respond because if he fought back people might get a negative impression about other black players who might enter the league. Public sentiment was incredibly important to further integration. However, once the shackles were taken off he became the MVP of the National League and a primary force for the Dodgers' first championship. It could be argued that Obama faced the same prejudice that those players did during his first term (at minimum). He presided during a period of divisiveness that is not altogether dissimilar from when the previous President from Illinois did. But once he won a second term, the gloves should have come completely off and we should have seen four years of an MVP-level president. Because he didn't, too many voters could not see the good he was doing. What they saw was someone trying to re-establish a status quo that had slowly been chipping away at their opportunities for a better life for the previous 30+ years. This was the first generation in US history that wasn't leaving their children in a better place than they had inherited. They were tired of the platitudes and tired of the same political rhetoric. They had been promised something different and now they wanted it. The problem with "different" is that just like eating sea urchin for the first time, different isn't always better. Sometimes it's just disgusting.

The racist backlash Obama has faced during his presidency
https://www.washingtonpost.com/graphics/national/obama-legacy/racial-backlash-against-the-president.html

Obama's effort to heal racial divisions and uplift black America
https://www.washingtonpost.com/graphics/national/obama-legacy/racism-during-presidency.html

Arms Control and Nonproliferation: A Catalog of Treaties and Agreements
https://crsreports.congress.gov/product/pdf/RL/RL33865

Russia, arms control and non-proliferation
https://www.europarl.europa.eu/RegData/etudes/BRIE/2020/652100/EPRS_BRI(2020)652100_EN.pdf

4 things to remember about Trump, Ukraine and Putin
https://www.cnn.com/2022/03/26/politics/trump-putin-ukraine/index.html

Abu Ghraib torture and prisoner abuse
https://en.wikipedia.org/wiki/Abu_Ghraib_torture_and_prisoner_abuse

Obama's Legacy: A Historic War On Whistleblowers
https://www.longislandpress.com/2017/01/14/obamas-legacy-historic-war-on-whistleblowers/

The "Versailles of Dresden" Has Been Rebuilt, 74 Years After World War II
https://www.smithsonianmag.com/smart-news/versaille-dresden-has-been-rebuilt-74-years-after-world-war-ii-180973225/

Exchange We Can Believe In
https://www.heritage.org/health-care-reform/commentary/exchange-we-can-believe

Why Conservatives Need a National Health Plan
https://www.heritage.org/political-process/report/why-conservatives-need-national-health-plan

A conservative think tank indignantly denies influencing Obamacare.
https://slate.com/news-and-politics/2010/04/the-conservative-heritage-foundation-indignantly-denies-influencing-obamacare.html#p2

Obama says Heritage Foundation is source of health exchange idea
https://www.politifact.com/factchecks/2010/apr/01/barack-obama/obama-says-heritage-foundation-source-health-excha/

The text of the Affordable Care Act, S.1770
https://www.govinfo.gov/content/pkg/BILLS-103s1770pcs/pdf/BILLS-103s1770pcs.pdf

Efforts to repeal the Affordable Care Act
https://en.wikipedia.org/wiki/Efforts_to_repeal_the_Affordable_Care_Act

Name the much-criticized federal program that has saved the U.S. $2.3 trillion. Hint: it starts with Affordable
https://www.statnews.com/2019/03/22/affordable-care-act-controls-costs/

Bill Gates Calls on the U.S. Government To Invest More in R&D
https://fortune.com/2016/04/18/bill-gates-oped-research-development/

Obama Has Done More for Clean Energy Than You Think
https://www.scientificamerican.com/article/obama-has-done-more-for-clean-energy-than-you-think/

The Obama solar success story that nobody talks about
https://whyy.org/articles/the-obama-solar-success-story-that-nobody-talks-about/

Feds Lend Tesla $465 Million to Build Model S
https://www.wired.com/2009/06/tesla-loan/

How China is Winning the Race for Clean Energy Technology
https://fairbank.fas.harvard.edu/research/blog/how-china-is-winning-the-race-for-clean-energy-technology%ef%bf%bc/

China Invests $546 Billion in Clean Energy, Far Surpassing the U.S.
https://www.scientificamerican.com/article/china-invests-546-billion-in-clean-energy-far-surpassing-the-u-s/

'Of course it could happen again': experts say little has changed since Deepwater Horizon
https://www.theguardian.com/environment/2020/apr/20/deepwater-horizon-10-years-later-could-it-happen-again

Reagan's Trump Card

Many old-school Republicans (and Democrats) will insist that Ronald Reagan would be horrified by Donald Trump. I disagree: Donald Trump is exactly what Reagan aspired to be.

Sure, Reagan talked about Social Security being sacrosanct but he quietly called anyone getting money from the government "free-loaders". He did everything he could to unburden the media from reporting facts and giving a platform to people who would say anything no matter how deceitful or ridiculous as long as it held a conservative viewpoint. He had contempt for anyone who brought up the downsides of siding with tyrants as long as they made good business partners (at least when it came to selling/buying weapons). He spit on the notion that markets should be regulated because what was in business' best interest was always what was in everyone else's best interest. He never sought the opinion of anyone who wasn't already wealthy unless they were also rabidly conservative. And he always maintained that whatever America did was always right simply because it was America that was doing it. There is nothing in that paragraph that doesn't also apply perfectly to Trump. Did I use the word "think" anywhere in there? Nope, so I got that right, too.

So let's start with his first year in office. He had zero legislative accomplishments. Sure, he signed 117 bills into law but 13% of those were dedicated to rolling back legislation Obama had enacted. To no one's surprise, he also wanted to repeal the ACA, with "something much better" but the three times he floated a "fix", he discovered that his "plan" would throw an additional 20 million Americans (at least) off their current healthcare. His biggest accomplishment was a tax cut for the wealthy and for corporations that to date has added $2 trillion to the deficit and is predicted to add another $1.5 trillion by 2033, with the majority of the tax burden being shifted toward the middle class over the next four years. Additionally, it further concentrated wealth for the top 10% of incomes, who now own more than 76% of all assets in the US. The bottom 50% own 1%, with 13 million families having a negative net worth.

The rest of Trump's "accomplishments" were the result of executive orders. He threatened to deport 800,000 American citizens (you read that right... nearly a million) by revoking DACA, a program that allowed children of illegal immigrants to remain in the country to get an education and become contributing citizens, which the vast majority have done. Within his first year in office, his Secretaries of Health, Veterans Affairs, Treasury, and EPA were all embroiled in scandals in which they wasted tens of millions of tax dollars using chartered and/or federal planes for personal business and other personal purposes. He blamed the mayor of San Juan, Puerto Rico for the damage caused by Hurricane Fiona while denying them, a US territory, any federal assistance because she had been critical of him. In a national security meeting, when the topic of hurricanes came up, he reportedly asked "Why can't we drop a nuke on them" when they're just forming off the coast of West Africa? Apparently, he wasn't aware of the true scale of a hurricane (hundreds of miles across where a nuclear detonation devastates roughly 10 miles radius) or the fact that one of the after-effects of a nuclear detonation is radioactive fallout that can be carried by the same winds that bring the hurricanes to our shores... only the fallout would then be swirling about at 150+ mph. He hired former General Michael Flynn, who had been an agent acting on behalf of the government of Turkey since 2014 and had ties to Vladimir Putin, to be one of his National Security Advisors. He held a nuclear strategy session in a public dining room. He appointed his daughter, two sons, and son-in-law, none of whom had any experience in government, to positions requiring top security clearance. He proposed a budget with a $2 trillion math error. He threatened nuclear war with North Korea. He withdrew the US from the Paris Climate Accord (because Obama had signed it). He used federal resources to advertise his personal properties and businesses (which is explicitly illegal) and refused to fill more than five hundred ambassadorial positions worldwide and more than two thousand White House positions. Trump's first year took Reagan's idea of a perfect smaller government to heart.

One of the things that Trump was supposed to bring to the office was unparalleled expertise in making deals. Never mind that almost every business he had ever owned had either gone bankrupt (even a casino!) or had its license revoked. He was supposed to win so much that we'd get tired of winning. One of the deals he "won" was a trade war with China to sell them beef. It only cost the American taxpayers $28 billion in farm subsidies while he stonewalled them in a tariff war. Meanwhile, the Chinese continue to make most of our electronics, and our clothes and are nearing a point where they'll hold a monopoly on solar power. So while the conservatives were popping champagne corks over a deal that sold a luxury item (which beef is surely becoming with how high the prices have gone), China will soon be holding monopoly interest on two of the fundamental necessities (clothing, energy) for human life. Well-played!!

Over the next two years, he routinely skipped intelligence briefings, instead preferring to get his news from Fox News talk shows, the same network that would pay a $787 million defamation settlement for lies they knowingly broadcast 24/7 about the 2020 election. His agency leaders seemed to have been hired either based on their antipathy toward the agency they were appointed to run, or their degree of unfamiliarity with what it was supposed to do...

For example, Betsy DeVos, the daughter of a billionaire who had been educated solely at Christian private schools and had spent her adult life campaigning against public school funding, instead favoring vouchers for private schooling and donating millions to those causes, was named Secretary of Education. Rick Perry, a former Republican Governor of Texas, had focused most of his political career on agriculture. He was named Secretary of Energy, despite not knowing that the Agency's primary responsibility was to manage our nuclear concerns (power plants, weapons, and their security). Greg Pruitt was named head of the Environmental Protection Agency. He was an economist with no scientific background whatsoever who had spent his entire career failing to debunk climate science and railing against the National Park System. Steve Mnuchin became Secretary of the Treasury despite being one of the financiers responsible for the 2007-08 meltdown. Wilbur Ross was named Secretary of Commerce, the same guy who had campaigned against minimum wages and health care guarantees. Ben Carson was named Secretary for Housing and Urban Development despite his vocal belief that poverty was merely a state of mind.

Speaking of poverty, Reagan was the first president since the introduction of the minimum wage not to raise it. Trump was the second. The minimum wage in 1980 was $3.35 per hour, which is equivalent to $13.22 per hour in today's dollars. The median income in 1980 was $16,400 ($64,725 today) and a minimum wage job would get you more than 40% there ($6,968, or about $27,500 today). Two parents working minimum wage jobs could earn almost 85% of the US median household income. The minimum wage under Obama was raised to today's rate of $7.25 ($15,080 per year). However, the median income is roughly $71,000. Today if two parents working minimum wage jobs have two kids, they qualify for federal poverty assistance.

As for the plantation owners, er, I mean the billionaires, the top 25 earned a combined $401 billion between 2014 and 2018 but paid an average of 3.6% of that in taxes. If you remove just their income from the pool (25 households out of nearly 130 million), the median income in the US drops by nearly a thousand dollars a year. In 1982, when Forbes first published its 400 wealthiest people list there were only about a dozen US billionaires; today there are 735, with 2640 worldwide. The lowest estimated worth on the list in 1982 was about $340 million in today's dollars; in 2019, the lowest net worth listed was $2.1 billion. The US now accounts for 40% of the world's millionaires.

Another Trump appointee was Jeff Sessions for the Attorney General despite having been deemed too racist by the Senate in his failed confirmation to become a district judge in Alabama under Reagan. Ironically, he refused to implement a travel ban on all Muslims entering the country and was summarily replaced by former Bush AG, William Barr. He covered for Trump's behavior many times, but perhaps his most famous occurred during Trump's first impeachment after appointing special counsel former FBI chief Robert Mueller to look into allegations of election meddling by Russia. Barr re-asserted a memo that declared a sitting president could not be prosecuted. Nevertheless, Mueller's investigation yielded at least seven instances where Trump had acted with both motive and opportunity to either solicit help from Russia or interfere with the investigation. Of course, nothing came of it because Mueller was not allowed to recommend indictments against a sitting president. Barr summarized the finding as exonerating Trump. A hyper-partisan Republican Congress then acquitted him.

Trump also appropriated $3.6 billion that had been earmarked to help military families pay for housing, schools, safety, and healthcare to instead pay for a wall to be built along the border with Mexico to keep out illegal immigrants. Never mind that the border ran through the middle of towns, through a river, and even through some people's houses. Or that upwards of 40% of those immigrants came to the US in planes and became "illegal" because they overstayed their visas. Or that since the invention of the wall, humans have also developed countermeasures to render them ineffective: explosives, siege engines, but on a more personal scale, power saws, tunnels, ladders, and ropes to name a few. As an aside, ropes predate walls by about 35,000 years. Yet another thing Trump and his followers evidently did not know.

Perhaps more interesting in all his anti-immigrant rhetoric is the fact that when people first immigrated to America, most were trying to get away from something: political or religious persecution, famine, tyrannical regimes. Now they come for work (41.7%) and for education (32.2%). There are 47 million immigrants in this country, roughly 14% of the population. In the most recent Census, only 57.8% of those asked identified themselves as white, which means that 42.2% came from somewhere else. Well, technically, 99.1% came from somewhere else because 0.9% are Native American or Native Hawaiian. That number might be higher as 4.1% identified as multi-racial. The point is that trying to "keep people out" is a little late at this point and a fundamentally flawed notion. It has never been a viable policy, especially considering the enormous contributions immigrants have made toward the success of this country.

Trump claimed that the media and the court system were the enemies of the people. From the hate crime murder of two Indian engineers to a political rally in Charlottesville in which one person was murdered, he refused to condemn racism, hate groups, or the violence that white supremacists increasingly engaged in. Far too many bought into the notion that the media was unfairly against him. They cited a Harvard Study of media reaction to Trump and previous presidents. It noted that CBS coverage of Trump was 91% negative. Negative reviews came from across the media spectrum: New York Times, 87% negative; the Washington Post, 83%; the Wall Street Journal, 70%. Even Fox News coverage also leaned to the negative, but only slightly: 52% negative to 48% positive. Even Fox News?!

But the study also stated, "Never in the nation's history, has the country had a president with so little fidelity to the facts, so little appreciation for the dignity of the presidential office, and so little understanding of the underpinnings of democracy." So the media wasn't being negative. They were simply reporting the things that he did, and normal people who are generally appalled by appalling things, were appalled. Funny how that works. When the facts proved the things he said so often were lies, it was their job to report that, too. That's not negative. That's honesty.

Speaking of honesty, scientists and epidemiologists had been warning of the inevitability of a deadly pandemic for decades. Laurie Garrett's 1994 best-seller The Coming Plague detailed several scenarios of how it would come about. The primary concerns were zoonotic disease (diseases that begin with animals but are transmitted to humans through contact), third-world conditions in much of the world, and the accessibility of rapid transport. The scientific consensus is that more than 60% of all human diseases are zoonotic and that 75% of all emerging infectious diseases come from livestock. Thirteen of those zoonoses, like rabies, hepatitis E, anthrax, sleeping sickness, and at least one form of tuberculosis just to name a few, are responsible for 2.2 million deaths per year. A study conducted in 2013 estimated that there are at least 320,000 different viruses that affect animals. If that seems like a high number consider the fact that the human digestive system has been found to contain more than 140,000 viruses (almost all of them benign, obviously) and that the number of different viruses on Earth is likely in the hundreds of millions. Not the number of them; the number of strains there are. So there was a likelihood that a more severe version of a disease like SARS in 2002, the swine flu in 2009, or Ebola in 2014 would evolve. There was so much concern that in 2014 Obama created a pandemic response team in the White House so that they could react quickly to such a threat. As part of "cost-cutting measures", Trump cut funding to the group, fired two-thirds of the staff, and had the rest transferred to other agencies. In addition, he cut CDC funding that helped prevention efforts in thirty-nine countries by 80%. One of the countries affected by the cut: China. In September of 2019, the White House Council of Economic Advisors handed him a report called "Mitigating the Impact of Pandemic Influenza through Vaccine Intervention". In it, they argued that existing private market solutions are unlikely to provide the necessary capability to handle such a threat, that the government needed to fund such efforts, and that the likely costs, both economic and loss of life, would be catastrophic if such efforts were not undertaken. They also strongly suggested that a large-scale vaccination program would be invaluable to combating such a threat. Trump ignored it.

In December 2019, an outbreak of a disease similar to SARS (the same kind of coronavirus) was detected in the Chinese city of Wuhan. It was thought to have originated in the wet markets of that city. There were 256 known cases in China by December 31, 2019. By the time human-to-human transmission was confirmed by the World Health Organization and Chinese disease authorities on January 20, 2020, there were 6,174 cases where people showed symptoms in China, South Korea, Thailand, and Japan, but many more were suspected to have been infected. On January 21, the first case was found in the US, as well as Vietnam and Singapore. On January 24, the WHO announced that the virus risk was high globally. Just two days before, Trump responded to a question at a press conference regarding COVID-19: "We have it totally under control. It's just one person coming from China. It's going to be just fine." He reiterated that same message the day the WHO report came out. By January 30, the number of cases worldwide had multiplied a hundred times over. On January 31, two confirmed cases were found in Italy. It was two tourists from China. WHO declared a world health emergency. At a rally in Iowa, Trump reaffirmed his previous stance, "We think we have it very well under control. We have very little problem in this country at this moment — five. ... we think it's going to have a very good ending for it.". He was urged to implement a complete travel ban to prevent further circulation but limited it to non-US residents who were coming from mainland China because it might hurt the economy. He eventually implemented a travel ban from Europe six weeks later in the middle of March.

By February 2, he was telling Fox News that, "We pretty much shut it down coming in from China."

On February 7, without any evidence to support his claim, he tweeted "virus hopefully becomes weaker with warmer weather, and then gone."

During a February 10 meeting with the US governors at the White House, he said, "A lot of people think that goes away in April with the heat — as the heat comes in. Typically, that will go away in April. We're in great shape, though. We have 12 cases — 11 cases, and many of them are in good shape now." Again, with no evidence to support such a claim.

He maintained that position throughout February, comparing it to the seasonal flu and that his administration had everything under control. He had already requested $1.25 billion in emergency aid to combat the virus, which ballooned to $8.3 billion in Congress by March 4. On February 29, the first US death from COVID-19 was recorded. It had already spread to every country in Europe.

Throughout March he continued to make false statements about his administration's response:

"If you want a test, you can get a test" – Production of tests had been delayed by mismanagement by his son-in-law, Jared Kushner, who wanted to apportion tests to states by whether they voted for Trump in the election. Despite promises that 1.5 million tests would be available, over the first 10 weeks, only 14,000 were administered.

"The health insurance industry agreed to waive all co-payments for coronavirus treatments" – They hadn't. Only the testing was covered.

"The WHO test is a bad test" – In fact, it was not. Independent labs had confirmed it was a valid test and Trump's own coordinator for coronavirus response assumed it was effective.

Trump claimed that Obama "didn't do anything about the swine flu" and that it was their negligence that made things so difficult. Both statements were blatantly false.

On March 17, he stated, "I've always known this is a real, this is a pandemic. I've felt it was a pandemic long before it was called a pandemic." That same day he asked people to work from home if they could, postpone unnecessary travel, and limit social gatherings to no more than ten people. A week later he was optimistic that things would be back to normal by Easter (April 12). By the end of the month, he finally acknowledged that there would be hard days ahead. On March 27, he signed the CARES (Coronavirus Aid, Relief and Economic Security) Act, which authorized $2.2 trillion in direct payments to citizens, payments to health care providers, tax credits and, what would become more controversial, a loan program called the Paycheck Protection Program (PPP) that would distribute $1.169 trillion to businesses, many of them large corporations. To date, more than $250 billion in fraudulent claims have been discovered from these relief funds. Additionally, more than 90% of the loans were eventually "forgiven".

Meanwhile, Kushner continued to mismanage federal resources, once referring to the PPE (masks and other safety equipment) and other medical supplies as "our stockpile" as if they were the Trump family's own. He bragged that Trump was "taking the country back from the doctors," and used a group of volunteers using their personal email accounts to buy more supplies for the federal government so that they could decide which states got them, either to the highest bidder or to the one's most eager to please Trump. This was all in April of 2020.

At the beginning of April, the number of American deaths due to COVID was less than 4,000. By April 11, the number had passed 20,000, surpassing Italy's total for most in the world outside of China. By the end of April, the number of deaths in the US had topped 50,000. That number would double by the end of May.

Trump added to the maelstrom of incompetence by suggesting (on April 4) that hydroxychloroquine (a drug for malaria treatment) might be a viable treatment despite no evidence. Several studies soon found that subjects developed an irregular heartbeat which prevented them from continuing, and a more recent study found that mortality increased by 11% from its use, resulting in an estimated additional 16,990 deaths by 2023. He stated (April 11) that he had "total authority" to lift quarantines when in fact the Constitution pretty explicitly delegates that power to the state governments. He urged states to "re-open" to get the economy going again. At an April 23 press conference, he suggested that getting disinfectant or ultraviolet light inside the body might help. At that same press conference, he urged states to re-open their schools. In May, he terminated relations with WHO because he claimed they "were pressured by China to mislead the world about the virus". All of WHO's statements to that point had proven true. In June, he claimed that "the numbers were up because our big number testing." When he made that statement, there were more than 2 million confirmed cases in the US and the death toll had surpassed 110,000. In April he had advocated people to use masks to prevent the spread; by August he was saying that masks were ineffective. They, in fact, do slow the spread of COVID and other air-borne diseases. Only one study has been cited that they might not and its findings state emphatically that the researchers could not find enough evidence to conclude one way or the other and that more study was needed. Over the next several months Trump continued to downplay the severity of both the disease and the spread.

The facts were that it was 10-20 times more lethal than the seasonal flu, and the death rate per capita in the United States was worse than all but twenty (out of 238) countries in the world. He blamed doctors for inflating numbers to get more money even though false reporting is a felony. Despite his own infection which required a week's stay at Walter Reed Hospital with round-the-clock medical attention, he campaigned around the country for re-election, insisting that the disease shouldn't "dominate your life", that we were "rounding the corner" and that a vaccine would be available to the public before Election Day. The first vaccine wasn't authorized by the FDA until December 11, one month after the election, and vaccinations weren't opened to everyone over age 16 until April 19, 2021.

Trump lost the election. On his final day in office, there were more than 24,000,000 cases in the US and more than 400,000 Americans had died from it. In March 2020, the same week Trump acknowledged that it might be bigger than the seasonal flu, a British study indicated that in the US there would be more than 2.2 million deaths without some kind of coordinated response. To date, the death toll in the US stands at more than 1.18 million, making it the deadliest event in US history, killing more Americans than either World War, the Civil War, or the H1N1 Flu Epidemic of 1917 (often called the Spanish Flu) which was a more virulent strain that killed an estimated fifty million worldwide and as many as 850,000 in the US. By comparison, the death toll for COVID-19 worldwide stands around seven million. A recent Lancet Study indicated that 40% of the US deaths could have been avoided with a competent organized response, citing numerous errors in judgment, lack of preparedness, and artificial shortfalls committed by Trump and his administrators for the higher-than-expected death toll.

Had that been the end of the Trump story, it would still rank as one of the worst episodes in US history. Outraged by his loss in the election by more than seven million votes, he expanded the claim that he had been floating for much of the year when polling numbers indicated that he might lose: that if he lost, it was because of election fraud. This was not the first time he had used election fraud as an excuse. In the 2016 election which he won on the electoral count, he lost the popular vote by more than two million votes. He claimed that there was widespread fraud and that five million of those votes had been cast by illegal immigrants. Of course, no proof was ever found or offered despite Trump convening a commission led by noted Republican advocate of anti-immigration laws and voter fraud investigations, Kris Kobach, to look into it. He found none. Trump disbanded the commission before it could submit an official report.

He assembled a legal team to fight the 2020 results in court. Sixty-two times his team brought his claim in circuit and appellate courts, more than a third of which were presided over by a judge that Trump had appointed. Every judge threw the suits out for lack of evidence. Any evidence. They had presented none. Two independent firms, both hired by Trump, confirmed that there had been no meaningful election fraud. Even the Supreme Court, which had six conservative justices, three of whom Trump had appointed, denied his appeal.

That didn't stop Trump from hosting a rally on January 6, 2021, the day the electoral count would be confirmed at the Capitol. In his speech, he implored those gathered that they might have to take matters into their own hands to protect the country. Spurred on by his admonition, the crowd marched from the White House to the Capitol steps, then violently pushed their way past Capital Police into the building, threatening to kill members of the House and the Vice President. Trump watched on television for three hours before finally heeding pleas from his staff to tell the demonstrators to stand down.

It was later discovered that:

1) Trump had tried to persuade the Secretary of State for Georgia to "find 11,780 extra votes" so he wouldn't lose that state,

2) that a scheme had been hatched in which the Republican National Committee would help Republican-led states appoint alternate electors whom the Vice President would use to replace the official electors during the official count. They would then cast their votes for Trump when the states had voted for Biden,

3) that he had a hand in organizing the insurrection at the Capitol (which was revealed during a Congressional Committee investigation of the attack) and

4) that he wanted to lead it.

Pence balked at the plan at the last minute so the "steal" never took place. It was also later revealed that Trump had discussed imposing martial law in the states he had lost to re-run the election there. However, that didn't stop 147 Republicans (139 in the House, 8 in the Senate) from voting to overturn the election and uphold the fake electors just hours after the Capitol was attacked.

If that wasn't enough, he also found the time to pardon the Blackwater operatives who had been convicted for the Nissour massacre in Iraq. Why? Because Erik Prince, the CEO of Blackwater, was Betsy DeVos' brother. Between his election loss and the day he had to vacate the White House, he had absconded with dozens of boxes filled with official documents, some of them classified as top secret including a potential war plan with Iran. He then refused to return them to the National Archives, even responding to a subpoena by the FBI claiming he no longer had them. After a year and a half of waiting for Trump to comply, the FBI served a warrant on his residence at Mar-a-Lago and recovered many of the documents.

To date, more than 378 conspirators in the January 6 insurrection have been sentenced, with more than 600 others awaiting sentencing. Beginning in March 2024, Trump is scheduled to be tried in four separate courts covering 91 federal indictments. Among the charges he faces are fraud, falsifying business records, racketeering, election interference, mishandling classified documents, and conspiracy to defraud the government. Nineteen people were charged in the Georgia case, with four already making plea deals and will testify in the other cases. As for the classified documents case, Trump was charged with a 37-

count indictment, including 30 violations of the Espionage Act. That trial is scheduled to begin in May of 2024.

To that end, perhaps the longest-lasting legacy of the Trump presidency will be his impact on the judiciary. All totaled, he appointed three Supreme Court justices (all of whom dissembled under oath during their confirmation hearings), 54 appeals court judges, and 174 district court judges, including eight that the American Bar Association deemed "unqualified", two of whom had never even tried a case as counsel. In addition, there were forty-six others whose nominations were so unqualified that even the Republican-controlled Senate had to refuse to hear them. It's hard to imagine a Presidential judicial nomination less qualified than someone who had never seen the inside of a courtroom.

Finally, there is the most troubling aspect and foreboding aspect of his presidency. Throughout his term, Trump routinely fired people for what he deemed as disloyalty or independence, rarely, if ever, for incompetence. He even floated the idea that all civil servants be forced to sign a loyalty pledge to him. Not his office. Him. A government's whole reason for existence is to serve the needs of the greatest number of people. A loyalty pledge to one man invalidates its reason for existing. Given Reagan's dislike of government, it's hard not to consider that he might have relished this idea. It's then altogether both fitting and ironic that a president who is responsible for the largest loss of lives in the country's history, who could realistically be charged with sedition and treason (the latter due to evidence that suggests he may have been used as an asset for Putin), who undermined the very essence of what it means to have a representative government and who labeled those who serve to protect it "suckers"… that he is the inevitable result of Reagan's vision. "The Great Communicator" might not have had this specifically in mind when he proposed any of his anti-government policies, but given the competitive nature of humans and the certainty that power corrupts, particularly when government power is put in private hands, it should not be at all surprising that this is where we ended up.

The history of 'rigged' US elections: from Bush v Gore to Trump v Clinton
https://www.theguardian.com/us-news/2016/oct/25/donald-trump-rigged-election-bush-gore-florida-voter-fraud

These are the bills Trump signed into law in his first year as President
https://www.cnn.com/2017/06/29/politics/president-trump-legislation/index.html

4 ways Trump's tax cuts changed the American economy
https://www.cnn.com/2019/04/15/economy/trump-tax-cuts-impact-economy/index.html

Extending Trump Tax Cuts Would Add $3.5 Trillion to the Deficit, According to CBO
https://www.budget.senate.gov/chairman/newsroom/press/extending-trump-tax-cuts-would-add-35-trillion-to-the-deficit-according-to-cbo

Has Wealth Inequality in America Changed over Time? Here Are Key Statistics
https://www.stlouisfed.org/open-vault/2020/december/has-wealth-inequality-changed-over-time-key-statistics

6 facts about economic inequality in the U.S.
https://www.pewresearch.org/short-reads/2020/02/07/6-facts-about-economic-inequality-in-the-u-s/

Did Trump Ask Advisers About 'Nuking' Hurricanes?
https://www.snopes.com/fact-check/trump-nuke-hurricanes/

President Trump Is Stealing From Military Families to Pay for His Border Wall Boondoggle
https://www.newsweek.com/president-trump-stealing-military-families-pay-his-border-wall-boondoggle-opinion-1458653

Report On The Investigation Into Russian Interference In The 2016 Presidential Election, Volume 1
https://www.justice.gov/storage/report_volume1.pdf

Report On The Investigation Into Russian Interference In The 2016 Presidential Election, Volume 2
https://www.justice.gov/storage/report_volume2.pdf

History of Federal Minimum Wage Rates Under the Fair Labor Standards Act, 1938 - 2009
https://www.dol.gov/agencies/whd/minimum-wage/history/chart

The Secret IRS Files: Trove of Never-Before-Seen Records Reveal How the Wealthiest Avoid Income Tax
https://www.propublica.org/article/the-secret-irs-files-trove-of-never-before-seen-records-reveal-how-the-wealthiest-avoid-income-tax

Income in the United States: 2021
https://www.census.gov/library/publications/2022/demo/p60-276.html

Number of US Households in 2024: Demographics, Statistics, & Trends
https://financesonline.com/number-of-us-households

Summary of the Latest Federal Income Tax Data, 2022 Update
https://taxfoundation.org/data/all/federal/summary-latest-federal-income-tax-data-2022-update/

Listing the Rich, Richer, Richest 400 in the U.S.
https://www.washingtonpost.com/archive/business/1982/08/28/listing-the-rich-richer-richest-400-in-the-us/e85b3960-77cd-4509-95ad-53bb259901e2/

Why do immigrants come to the US?
https://usafacts.org/articles/why-do-people-immigrate-us/

What Is the 2024 Federal Poverty Level (FPL)?
https://smartasset.com/financial-advisor/federal-poverty-level-2020

Racial and Ethnic Diversity in the United States: 2010 Census and 2020 Census
https://www.census.gov/library/visualizations/interactive/racial-and-ethnic-diversity-in-the-united-states-2010-and-2020-census.html

Zoonotic Diseases: Etiology, Impact, and Control
https://www.ncbi.nlm.nih.gov/pmc/articles/PMC7563794/

How many viruses on Earth?
https://virology.ws/2013/09/06/how-many-viruses-on-earth/

Scientists identify more than 140,000 virus species in the human gut
https://www.sciencedaily.com/releases/2021/02/210218142739.htm

13 Animal-to-Human Diseases Kill 2.2 Million People Each Year
https://www.livescience.com/21426-global-zoonoses-diseases-hotspots.html

Mitigating the Impact of Pandemic Influenza through Vaccine Innovation
https://trumpwhitehouse.archives.gov/wp-content/uploads/2019/09/Mitigating-the-Impact-of-Pandemic-Influenza-through-Vaccine-Innovation.pdf

A Strategy To Estimate Unknown Viral Diversity in Mammals
https://journals.asm.org/doi/10.1128/mbio.00598-13

Did Obama Urge US Pandemic Preparedness in 2014?
https://www.snopes.com/fact-check/obama-pandemic-preparedness-2014/

Did Trump Administration Fire the US Pandemic Response Team?
https://www.snopes.com/fact-check/trump-fire-pandemic-team/

White House Economists Warned in 2019 a Pandemic Could Devastate America
https://www.nytimes.com/2020/03/31/business/coronavirus-economy-trump.html

Novel Coronavirus (2019-nCoV) SITUATION REPORT – 4 - 24 JANUARY 2020
https://www.who.int/docs/default-source/coronaviruse/situation-reports/20200124-sitrep-4-2019-ncov.pdf?sfvrsn=9272d086_8

Statement on the second meeting of the International Health Regulations (2005) Emergency Committee regarding the outbreak of novel coronavirus (2019-nCoV)
https://www.who.int/news-room/detail/30-01-2020-statement-on-the-second-meeting-of-the-international-health-regulations-(2005)-emergency-committee-regarding-the-outbreak-of-novel-coronavirus-(2019-ncov)

All The Times Trump Compared Covid-19 To The Flu, Even After He Knew Covid-19 Was Far More Deadly
https://www.forbes.com/sites/tommybeer/2020/09/10/all-the-times-trump-compared-covid-19-to-the-flu-even-after-he-knew-covid-19-was-far-more-deadly/?sh=6b393040f9d2

How Jared Kushner's Secret Testing Plan "Went Poof Into Thin Air"
https://www.vanityfair.com/news/2020/07/how-jared-kushners-secret-testing-plan-went-poof-into-thin-air

Behind the scenes, Kushner takes charge of coronavirus response
https://www.politico.com/news/2020/04/01/jared-kushner-coronavirus-response-160553

Kushner's coronavirus team shied away from a national strategy, believing that the virus was hitting Democratic states hardest and that they could blame governors, report says
https://www.businessinsider.com/kushner-covid-19-plan-maybe-axed-for-political-reasons-report-2020-7?op=1

"That's Their Problem": How Jared Kushner Let the Markets Decide America's COVID-19 Fate
https://www.vanityfair.com/news/2020/09/jared-kushner-let-the-markets-decide-covid-19-fate

Jared Kushner's Role In Coronavirus Response Draws Scrutiny, Criticism
https://www.npr.org/2020/04/04/826922646/jared-kushners-role-in-coronavirus-response-draws-scrutiny-criticism

An explosive documentary details how Jared Kushner's coronavirus task force consisted mainly of 20-something volunteers buying PPE with personal email accounts
https://www.businessinsider.com/documentary-all-under-control-kushner-task-force-2020-10-07?op=1

Jared Kushner bragged in April that Trump was taking the country 'back from the doctors'
https://www.cnn.com/2020/10/28/politics/woodward-kushner-coronavirus-doctors/index.html

Hydroxychloroquine
https://en.wikipedia.org/wiki/Hydroxychloroquine

Revisiting the initial COVID-19 pandemic projections
https://www.thelancet.com/journals/lanmic/article/PIIS2666-5247(21)00029-X/fulltext

List of human disease case fatality rates
https://en.wikipedia.org/wiki/List_of_human_disease_case_fatality_rates

Estimating the COVID-19 infection fatality ratio accounting for seroreversion using statistical modelling
https://www.nature.com/articles/s43856-022-00106-7

Mortality Risk of COVID-19
https://ourworldindata.org/mortality-risk-covid

Timeline: How Donald Trump responded to the coronavirus pandemic
https://www.politifact.com/article/2020/mar/20/how-donald-trump-responded-coronavirus-pandemic/

COVID-19 pandemic death rates by country
https://en.wikipedia.org/wiki/COVID-19_pandemic_death_rates_by_country

COVID-19 vaccination in the United States
https://en.wikipedia.org/wiki/COVID-19_vaccination_in_the_United_States

Damning analysis of Trump's pandemic response suggested 40% of US COVID-19 deaths could have been avoided
https://www.businessinsider.com/analysis-trump-covid-19-response-40-percent-us-deaths-avoidable-2021-2?op=1

Here's How Many COVID Deaths We Can Blame on Trump's Terrible Response
https://www.vice.com/en/article/k7a57v/heres-how-many-covid-deaths-we-can-blame-on-trumps-terrible-response

Deaths induced by compassionate use of hydroxychloroquine during the first COVID-19 wave: an estimate
https://www.sciencedirect.com/science/article/pii/S075333222301853X

Mortality outcomes with hydroxychloroquine and chloroquine in COVID-19 from an international collaborative meta-analysis of randomized trials
https://www.nature.com/articles/s41467-021-22446-z

'Biggest fraud in a generation': The looting of the Covid relief plan known as PPP
https://www.nbcnews.com/politics/justice-department/biggest-fraud-generation-looting-covid-relief-program-known-ppp-n1279664

Virtually all PPP loans have been forgiven with limited scrutiny
https://www.npr.org/2022/10/12/1128207464/ppp-loans-loan-forgiveness-small-business

How the Paycheck Protection Program went from good intentions to a huge free-for-all
https://www.npr.org/2023/01/09/1145040599/ppp-loan-forgiveness

How well do face masks protect against COVID-19?
https://www.mayoclinic.org/diseases-conditions/coronavirus/in-depth/coronavirus-mask/art-20485449

Select January 6th Committee Final Report and Supporting Materials Collection
https://www.govinfo.gov/collection/january-6th-committee-final-report?path=/GPO/January%206th%20Committee%20Final%20Report%20and%20Supporting%20Materials%20Collection

Presidential Advisory Commission on Election Integrity
https://en.wikipedia.org/wiki/Presidential_Advisory_Commission_on_Election_Integrity

The 59 worst things Trump did during his presidency
https://www.indy100.com/news/donald-trump-worst-moments-president-2664003687

The 10 Worst Things Trump Did in 2020
https://www.aei.org/op-eds/the-10-worst-things-trump-did-in-2020/

The Republicans who voted to overturn the election
https://www.reuters.com/graphics/USA-TRUMP/LAWMAKERS/xegpbedzdvq/

The 147 Republicans Who Voted to Overturn Election Results
https://www.nytimes.com/interactive/2021/01/07/us/elections/electoral-college-biden-objectors.html

Trump assembles a ragtag crew of conspiracy-minded allies in flailing bid to reverse election loss
https://www.washingtonpost.com/politics/trump-assembles-a-ragtag-crew-of-conspiracy-minded-allies-in-flailing-bid-to-reverse-election-loss/2020/12/21/d7674cd2-43b2-11eb-b0e4-0f182923a025_story.html

Chronicling Trump's 10 worst abuses of power
https://www.cnn.com/2021/01/24/politics/trump-worst-abuses-of-power/index.html

The Trump 2020 impact report: 10 ways the president has changed America
https://www.theguardian.com/us-news/2019/dec/31/trump-2020-impact-report-environment-america

Donald Trump nominates lawyer who has never tried a case for lifetime federal judgeship
https://www.independent.co.uk/news/world/americas/donald-trump-judge-nominee-brett-talley-senate-judiciary-committee-no-trial-experience-alabama-horror-novels-blogger-a8051741.html

The Senate Just Confirmed a Trump Judge With No Real Trial or Litigation Experience
https://www.esquire.com/news-politics/politics/a30140278/trump-judge-confirmed-sarah-pitlyk-no-trial-experience/

John Bolton: Trump Is a Putin-Loving Moron Who Thought Finland Was Part of Russia
https://www.vanityfair.com/news/2022/03/john-bolton-donald-trump-ukraine-finland-russia

Reversing Course?

That just about brings us to where we are now.

It is unfortunate that we can't talk about the current President, Joe Biden, without also having to spend more time on Donald Trump. At the behest of the former president, the Republicans in Congress conducted three investigations into Biden in an attempt to impeach him. To date, they have no evidence of wrongdoing despite absurd efforts to find some. In fact, the only witness they had turned out to be a Russian asset. Whoops. Among their purported "scandals" are (and I'm not making this up): a text message from his son, Hunter, asking for money to help him cover his alimony payments, a check from Hunter for $1380 with "car payment" in the subject line, and Hunter's laptop, which they claimed would contain national secrets. After months of bloviating about it harboring data that would undo this presidency, the most scandalous reveals were some photos of Hunter naked. There were a few of him posing with a gun, which led to an illegal possession charge, but this was not exactly the evidence of treason that was promised to Trump's rabid followers. Since Hunter isn't an elected official, nor did the President appear in any of the photos, and the timeline for all of their accusations is placed during a span when the President was not holding any office and had yet to declare himself as a candidate for president, this was all just more Gingrich-ian foul air. The whole impeachment effort has been a pathetic attempt to show that both parties are corrupt. The reasoning stands that if both Trump and Biden had been impeached, at least Trump was entertaining. Only they aren't, they haven't and he's not. The man leading the "investigations", Republican Congressman James Comey, is doing his best Newt Gingrich impression by now being investigated for the very crimes he has accused Biden of committing.

Controversially, that same Congress has offered no investigation into Jared Kushner's post-administration payment of $2 billion from Saudi Arabia's Crown Prince Mohammed bin Salman, reportedly for providing intelligence to Saudi operatives about opposition leaders, including a Washington Post journalist and critic of the Saudi regime named Jamal Khashoggi who was murdered and dissected on bin Salman's orders.

Also stuck in Trump's stasis field are his criminal trials, which have been delayed by at least a year due to the inaction of Biden's Attorney General, Merrick Garland. As an aside, why is it that most of the Attorney Generals over the last 50+ years have been abysmal at upholding the law? Beginning with Nixon we have had:

John Mitchell (Nixon): *led* the Watergate break-in and cover-up, and went to prison.

Richard Kleindienst (Nixon): convicted of contempt of Congress over the Watergate affair.

Robert Bork (Nixon): while technically not an AG, he was acting as one when he fired special prosecutor Archibald Cox during the Watergate investigation after Elliot Richardson and William Rucklshaus both refused and resigned over Nixon's order. Bork was later nominated to the Supreme Court by Reagan, but his nomination failed.

Ed Meese (Reagan): involved in several "ethical lapses" helping companies in which he was vested, he argued there were no hungry children in America, but did spend time and government money compiling a report that maintained pornography was going to ruin it. He also thought that reading someone their Miranda Rights was a waste of time: "You don't have many suspects who are innocent of a crime."

John Ashcroft (Bush 2): Ignored warnings of an imminent Al Queda attack, green-lighted torture, er, I mean, enhanced interrogation techniques.

Alberto Gonzales (Bush 2): continued Ashcroft's torture policies, denied that Article 1 of the Constitution protected citizens from unlawful detention (it does and has been ruled that way literally thousands of times), fired seven Republican US federal prosecutors for prosecuting too many Republicans. It turns out they were prosecuting the right people as most of their targets were later convicted. Two of the seven were fired because Bush wanted someone with similar ideologies to his in place, and another was fired so that an aide to Karl Rove, Bush's Chief of Staff, could have a better job.

Eric Holder (Obama): like Kleindienst, found guilty of contempt of Congress, vowed to continue prosecutions for marijuana possession even in states that legalized it. He also gave the go-ahead for drone strikes of suspected terrorists even though many others were captured and convicted using the court system. But sure, make a mockery of the international prohibition against assassinations.

Bill Barr (Bush 2, Trump): *also* found guilty of contempt of Congress, actively thwarted the investigation of BCCI (a case that centered around a bank that was eventually found guilty of fraud and money laundering for organized crime, several foreign governments and their intelligence agencies), authored a report that grossly cherry-picked data sets advocating for increased incarceration rates which stated (and I'm not making this up) "the benefits of increased incarceration would be enjoyed disproportionately by black Americans", counseled the 1st Bush to pardon the convicted participants in the Iran-Contra affair so that Bush would not have to testify at Caspar Weinberger's trial, perverted the findings of the Mueller Report (which might also be construed as obstruction of justice) and ran cover for *all* of Trump's questionable and illegal activity from 2019-2020, including parroting his concerns about election integrity through the election. It wasn't until after his investigation into "voting irregularities" in the states Trump lost concluded and yielded *no* evidence of fraud that he finally, on December 1, one month after the election, announced that there was no election fraud.

Jeff Sessions (Trump, preceding Barr): lied under oath about having contact with members of the Russian government during the 2016 campaign, revived the policy of civil asset forfeiture of property from suspects who are not yet charged with a crime, implemented a policy where police departments accused of committing certain crimes would not be investigated.

Merrick Garland (Biden): legally, he hasn't done anything in violation of the law but his foot-dragging with all of the Trump investigations has put unnecessary stress on the legal system due to the limited time frame before the 2024 election. He claimed he didn't want to inject politics into the elections, but 1) upholding the law is *not* a political act, and 2) by *not* acting when evidence demanded it, he made a political decision thereby accomplishing the opposite of his stated intention. But honestly, as a long-time member of of the Federalist Society, none of what he's done (and not done) should be surprising.

But enough prologue… after his first three years as President, it appears that Joe Biden will be something we haven't seen in a long time: a leader with a real focus on the future. In his first State of the Union address, he spoke about the government being "us" and not some abstract entity that interferes in our lives from afar. So far he's delivered on that promise. He has embraced the idea, as FDR put it, "that the job of the government is to create economic upturns." Despite being limited by a historically contentious House of Representatives that might go down as one of the least productive ever, he has managed to pass significant funding for infrastructure, manufacturing (particularly in the technology sector), green energy, COVID relief, reducing child poverty and providing military and humanitarian aid for Ukraine in their defense against Putin's invasion. He's forgiven the student loan debt of 3.75 million Americans, totaling more than $138 billion, thereby setting them on a more manageable path to prosperity.

All of these had their roots in Reagan's policies. He and his followers had no problem letting manufacturing jobs get exported. They had no problem cutting funding for infrastructure. They actively subsidized the fossil fuels industry. They also believed poverty was a choice. And student debt was something Reagan actively campaigned for.

When he was running for Governor of California, one of his advisors was an economist named Roger Freeman. He had been an economic advisor to both Eisenhower and Nixon and had spent his career fighting against public education, welfare programs, and other government services. When Reagan was looking for ways to cut the state budget, Freeman argued that he should cut funding for the state universities, which were considered among the best, if not the best, in the country despite being tuition-free. The Civil Rights Act opened the doors so that anyone, including people of color and women, could get a free college education in California. Reagan hated the activism he saw on the campuses and blamed it on diversity. He felt another barrier needed to be placed to weed out the people he viewed as undesirables. "We made it plain that tuition must be accompanied by adequate loans to be paid back after graduation," he campaigned in 1966. Freeman went a step further, stating, "We are in danger of producing an educated proletariat," using Marx's term for the working class. He continued, "That's dynamite! We have to be selective about who we allow to go through higher education." Reagan carried that policy with him to the White House. Student debt grew 25% during just Reagan's administration. Public funding of state universities dropped by 25% over the subsequent two decades, which meant colleges were increasingly dependent on endowments from the wealthy, who in turn, demanded preferential treatment and favors to secure more funding. Tuition rates increased by 260% from 1990-2020. In 1975, Pell Grants covered nearly 80% of the costs to attend a public four-year college. Today, Pell Grants pay for less than 30%, leaving students with little option besides loans to pay for the most affordable option. So yeah, Reagan was the one who created the $1.5 trillion student debt problem. Hooray for the capitalists who pulled up the same ladder they used to get to the top, then heaped condescension on everyone who followed for not working hard enough!

But back to Biden... he also enacted the first significant laws regarding gun safety in a quarter century. He passed additional funding for the IRS which has resulted in more than $500 billion reclaimed in back taxes from the wealthy. That one is huge because it has the promise of restoring some sanity to our current tax system. It is estimated that more than $4 trillion in untaxed wealth has been sequestered away in overseas tax havens, and hundreds of billions have been stashed in domestic trusts. Another sector of tax avoidance that bears closer scrutiny is non-profit organizations, also known as 501(c)(3) corporations.

When the tax code governing their administration was written in 1913, there were roughly 12,000 non-profit organizations in the US, including churches, making up about 1% of the total workforce. Today there are more than 1.48 million of them, not including more than 400,000 churches. Non-profits employ more than 10% of the workforce and report an annual revenue of $2.62 trillion and assets totaling more than $1.1 trillion. Not bad for being "non-profit". The vast majority of that change came between 1981 and 2004. What happened during that period? Changes in the tax laws by both Reagan and Clinton allowed the wealthy to buy assets like multi-million dollar houses and artworks, then "donate" them to non-profit foundations they control. In exchange for the tax breaks, these assets are supposed to be available for public viewing but far more often than not never are. Political Action Committees or PACs also fall under this tax classification, as do "think tanks", like the Heritage Foundation. They were one of the big proponents of the Star Wars initiative as well as the Republican "culture wars", which blamed ethnic cultural influences (not the economic system) for the increasing division and inequality.

Biden put a cap on the consumer prices for ten medications after Bush's Medicare Part D plan closed a coverage loophole but forbade the government from negotiating the price of medications. Since 1984, drug prices have outpaced inflation by 300%. The genesis of that increase came in 1983 when Reagan changed the way hospitals and doctors were reimbursed by Medicare. Whereas before, Medicare payments were tied to costs. He shifted the risk to the providers. So instead of Medicare covering the cost depending on each individual procedure, he decided there should only be a flat reimbursement based on the type. That incentivized hospitals and doctors to prioritize profit over the health of the patient. If an operation risked possible complications and thus the added expenses of dealing with them, why would a hospital or a doctor assume that risk as well as a potential malpractice suit if it didn't yield positive results, even if it was the only way to save the patient? That also opened the door to an increase in "out-patient services" which previously had required hospital stays.

It was also during Reagan's administration that direct-to-consumer marketing of prescription pharmaceuticals was allowed for the first time since 1962. Before him, prescription drug companies could only market to physicians, who understood how the medicines worked and thus were able to decide what would be right for their patients. Reagan felt that you didn't need to go to medical school to understand how medicine worked, so he relaxed those standards to allow drug makers to advertise directly to consumers. This was further increased in 1997 by a Clinton decision to allow the ads to be placed on television. So if you've ever felt like punching your own face because you can't get the Ozempic jingle out of your head, or wish the pharmaceutical industry would do something useful with the $7 billion they spend yearly on advertising, like convincing people that vaccines don't put microscopic mind-control robots in your head, now you know who to thank. As a result, the price of heart disease drugs (which treat the #1 cause of death in America) have increased by 1350% and make up 25% of the top 200 drugs prescribed in America. Biden has signaled that he'd like to reverse that trend putting forth a plan to force pharmaceutical companies to lower prices on medications that were developed using taxpayers' money, which includes all 356 drugs developed over the last decade, covering an investment of $230 billion.

Rampant inflation was also something that Biden had to deal with. The primary drivers for the inflation were somewhat obvious: more than a trillion dollars in PPP loans that Trump and Biden forgave, $4.5 in toxic assets, and qualitative easing that Obama had to offer to clean up George Bush's and Bill Clinton's misadventures in the financial markets, more than $3 trillion tax cuts from Trump and Bush, plus another $1.5 trillion from Bush's unfunded Iraq war… that's $10 trillion outstanding on an economy that runs about $22 trillion a year. Flagrant corporate price gouging under the cover of inflation didn't help. If you have been wondering why groceries have become so expensive, now you know. Collectively since 2022 nearly $100 billion in fines and settlements for price fixing have been levied against large corporations including several that produce food. Nineteen of those companies have been fined more than $1 billion *each* for screwing over consumers.

He's also proposed legislation that will force the hedge fund industry to relinquish all its holdings in single-family real estate. After the 2008 meltdown, institutional investors increasingly bought available single-family homes to turn them into rentals. In some markets, they control more than 25% of the inventory, driving both rental rates and purchase prices higher. He also directed his Consumer Financial Protection Bureau to crack down on junk fees, like overdraft fees, termination charges, and hotel booking fees that cost consumers more than $190 billion per year. Through all this chaos, Biden and his Federal Reserve Chairman Jerome Powell have somehow managed to bring down inflation without shocking the system into the recession that most economists predicted was a certainty. As a result, job and wage growth have increased by historic amounts.

His appointments of Lina Khan at the FTC and three of the four members of the National Labor Relations Board and their General Counsel have revitalized those agencies. While Khan's lawsuits against tech giants Meta and Microsoft have failed to move conservative justices to rightly apply anti-trust statutes, she has focused on the right players to target. Biden's NLRB has re-energized the union movement. The successful strikes by the United Auto Workers and the Screenwriters Guild have sparked many unions across a broad range of industries to push for better wages and conditions because they now know the arbitration tables won't be tilted against them as they have been since Reagan. When Reagan took office, union membership was around 23% of the workforce. By the time he left, it was around 15% and dropping. It bottomed out at 10.1% in 2021 but the Bureau of Labor Statistics reported a recent uptick in membership despite more than half the states having "right to work" laws that make it extremely difficult for workers to unionize.

Deb Haaland at the Department of Interior is the first Native American appointed to a cabinet-level position and she is doing more to protect the people who were here before all the immigrants showed up than all previous interior secretaries combined. Among her accomplishments are getting more than $1.5 billion in water rights settlements and projects, and the creation of a new unit of the Bureau of Indian Affairs that will be focused solely on an unaddressed problem that has existed for nearly a century: missing or murdered Native Americans. That might not seem like a huge deal because it doesn't get much media attention, but the figures from a recent Department of Interior survey are jaw-dropping: 84.3% of Native American women have experienced physical violence in their lifetime and 56.1% have experienced sexual violence. Only 2% of the Native Americans reported missing were ever logged into the National

Missing and Unidentified Persons System, a research system maintained by the Department of Justice. Those are not misprints.

Given that information is even more readily available than ever due to the internet and the dramatic rise in youth activism, he has not been afforded the leeway previous presidents have had in supporting reactionary regimes that have historically been friendly to US interests. As an example, every President has been overly supportive of Israel since 1947, almost to a fault. But the conflict in Gaza has laid bare that supporting Benjamin Netanyahu's Zionist unrepentant aspirations to level Gaza in the name of Israeli defense is a non-starter for young voters, who have driven Democratic successes in the last two elections. He faces the unenviable task of trying to appease Jewish voters, who historically have been drivers of Democrats' successes, by supporting Israel while also trying to appease the youth and Arab-American vote, drivers of the Democrats' current success, by rebuffing Israel's over-reach.

Before anyone accuses me of being a Biden cheerleader, I'd like to make it clear that his unwavering support of Bush's war in Iraq and his rejection of Anita Hill's testimony during the Clarence Thomas confirmation hearings will forever be black marks on his character. Those were catastrophically bad decisions that had wholly predictable results and have imperiled thousands of Americans. It's highly unlikely he'll likely ever be the 21st-century FDR because he simply won't step on the necessary number of corporate toes to enact those kinds of sweeping reforms. The fact that he is often portrayed as "liberal" by the mainstream media shows just how unbalanced our national discourse has become.

But is this finally a reversal of Reagan's America?

The signs are certainly there. But even if it were obvious, I'm not sure many would notice enough to celebrate. Between the intellectual cesspool that is social media, what passes for journalism in today's click-bait mainstream news, and the propaganda engines that have been created over the last decade, Biden could personally cure cancer, colonize Mars, and play an earth-shaking drum solo for a Led Zeppelin reunion concert, yet the public reaction would undoubtedly be a monotone, "So what. It's just fake news. Probably AI or CGI or something."

Much of this apathy is due to the growing influence of social media on political opinion. The three most popular platforms are Meta, Twitter and TikTok. Meta was a key player in the Cambridge Analytica disinformation campaign that helped Donald Trump win in 2016. TikTok is state-owned by China. Twitter (now called "X") is owned by Elon Musk, a right-wing, self-proclaimed "free-speech absolutist" who has re-instated the accounts of actual Nazis, White Supremacists, and convicted propagandists while banning the accounts of mainstream journalists and silencing accounts critical of authoritarian regimes. But at least he's cracking down on child porn. Maybe. Musk himself has parroted the talking points of Vladimir Putin as well as numerous debunked conspiracy theories.

One of the rising stars of this confluence of ignorance and disinformation is former hedge fund manager Vivek Ramaswamy. Vivek made his money buying orphaned drugs from major pharmaceutical companies that couldn't make it past the first two trial phases, re-testing them with cherry-picked results, then hawking them as the next cure for diseases like Alzheimer's. Once investors bought millions in stock, he dumped his shares before the inevitable failure at the next drug trial. One of his most popular policy talking points is the idea that we need to reduce the federal workforce by 75%, and/or limit everyone's tenure as a federal worker to eight years. Fundamentally, it's about as frivolous and half-witted a proposal as can be imagined, especially since our national defense falls under that category. "Yeah, I'd like to apply for a job as a Major General. My work experience? I have been a waiter at Applebee's for the last three years but I play a lot of Call of Duty on my Xbox."

The turnover rate is very low among government employees and that's a good thing. Your food is safe because of federal standards set by scientists and researchers who determine expiration time frames, product safety procedures, transportation and storage requirements, and production standards that include sanitary minimum standards, and enforced by inspectors who make sure those standards are followed. Without those protections, we'd devolve back 150 years when vendors sold rancid meat and spoiled milk. FYI, food poisoning was one of the highest causes of mortality at the time. If you ever fly on an airplane, your flight is directed by teams of air traffic controllers, flight safety is determined by inspectors and the airports themselves are constructed, maintained, and used within very strict standards that are universally applied so that every time a pilot takes off or lands he knows that his plane is not gonna crash from the runway collapsing over soft ground or from a landing strip that has potholes. Fuel standards are strictly regulated so that pilots know their engines won't flame out or die in mid-air because of inconsistent fuel blends. Your highways are built to weather specifications for their geography. The federal government tests numerous grades and mixtures of asphalt so that the one that is laid down by federal contractors won't contribute to rubber melting or excessive skidding in the rain, snow, or ice. Your house is built to government standards so that the materials are uniform and the way they are constructed is inspected and approved by licensed individuals who are qualified to build a home that will remain safe. Your appliances are tested for safety and meet a federal minimum standard. The government maintains two dozen GPS satellites so your phone can give you directions. And I've already covered the sheer volume of government-sponsored scientific research and innovation that is given to you for free. Even more is bought by private enterprise for pennies on the dollar and sold back to you for outrageous profits. AccuWeather forecasts, for example, get their weather data from the National Weather Service for free, then sells it to you through cable contracts and other services.

Ronald Reagan liked to say that the nine most dangerous words in the English language are, "I'm from the government and I'm here to help." It was cute and catchy when he first said it, but it should be obvious by now to anyone who has been paying attention over the last forty years that after three financial meltdowns and their subsequent taxpayer-funded bailouts, an unfunded war against a country that had absolutely nothing to do with the worst terrorist attack in human history, and a pandemic that killed more Americans than any event in our 247 years of existence, that perhaps the government does have a particularly important role to play in our success, especially when it comes to regulating the behavior of the powerful. That role must be expanded through our participation. It can not be left to others to govern because that only opens to door for charlatans and opportunists who seek only to self-gratify.

Over the last seven years, it can be said that the United States has reached a critical juncture. Only once before has the political discourse been this rancorous and divided. The result then was a bloody Civil War. It is not a foregone conclusion that we'll end up in that same cauldron of blood. We have a choice but it requires everyone to embrace something that President Biden said in his State of the Union: "The government is us."

We decide which direction this country will go. We decide whether everyone will have access to affordable healthcare and autonomy over their health decisions and a right to vote without prejudice. We decide whether our taxpayer dollars will be used to support despots or to defend freedom, or to provide a proper education rather than subsidies for the super-rich. We decide. Of course, it took forty years to get into this predicament so it might require forty years to get out of it.

The Roman statesman and philosopher Cicero is credited with saying "Blessed are those who plant trees under whose shade they will never sit." Given the increasingly dire direction our planet is headed concerning climate change, that is quite literally a good idea. But metaphorically speaking, for us 21st-century

Americans, perhaps it is time we each start planting some trees of our own.

AOC Busts GOP Rep Cold 'Fabricating' Hunter Biden Evidence Live During Impeachment Hearing
https://www.msn.com/en-us/news/politics/aoc-busts-gop-rep-cold-fabricating-hunter-biden-evidence-live-during-impeachment-hearing/ar-AA1hrvJI

House Oversight GOP release document showing payments made by Hunter Biden to his dad; documents say they were for a car
https://www.cnn.com/2023/12/04/politics/oversight-committee-hunter-biden-car-payments/index.html

MBS DODGES question on wealth fund's $2B injection into Jared Kushner's private equity - as he admits 'mistakes' in killing of Jamal Khashoggi that CIA says he 'approved' and warns Saudi Arabia will get NUKES if Iran does
https://www.dailymail.co.uk/news/article-12542831/MBS-DODGES-question-wealth-funds-2B-injection-Jared-Kushners-private-equity-admits-mistakes-killing-Jamal-Khashoggi-CIA-says-approved-warns-Saudi-Arabia-NUKES-Iran-does.html

House Elects Mike Johnson as Speaker, Embracing a Hard-Right Conservative
https://www.nytimes.com/2023/10/25/us/politics/house-republicans-speaker-vote-johnson.html

Biden's accomplishments match up well with well-regarded former presidents
https://chicago.suntimes.com/2022/8/28/23325019/president-joe-biden-franklin-roosevelt-lyndon-johnson-ronald-reagan

Reagan, Deregulation and America's Exceptional Rise in Health Care Costs
https://www.nytimes.com/2018/06/04/upshot/reagan-deregulation-and-americas-exceptional-rise-in-health-care-costs.html

Direct-to-Consumer Advertising of Drugs
https://journalofethics.ama-assn.org/article/direct-consumer-advertising-drugs/2013-11

Biden-Harris Administration Announces Nearly $5 Billion in Additional Student Debt Relief
https://www.ed.gov/news/press-releases/biden-harris-administration-announces-nearly-5-billion-additional-student-debt-relief

How the Threat of an 'Educated Proletariat' Created the Student Debt Crisis
https://www.bestcolleges.com/news/analysis/threat-of-educated-proletariat-created-the-student-debt-crisis/

"The Demise of Higher Education in the United States"
https://economistsview.typepad.com/economistsview/2012/04/the-demise-of-higher-education-in-the-united-states.html

$4 Trillion In US Wealth Is Stashed Overseas, Much Of It In Tax Havens
https://www.taxpolicycenter.org/taxvox/4-trillion-us-wealth-stashed-overseas-much-it-tax-havens

How the Ultrawealthy Use Private Foundations to Bank Millions in Tax Deductions While Giving the Public Little in Return
https://www.propublica.org/article/how-private-nonprofits-ultrawealthy-tax-deductions-museums-foundation-art

Hedge Fund Housing Ban: A Game-Changer For The US Single-family Home Market?
https://www.msn.com/en-us/money/news/hedge-fund-housing-ban-a-game-changer-for-the-us-single-family-home-market/ar-AA1lftIC

2023 Junk fees report: impact on the American consumer
https://www.switchful.com/report/junk-fees

When a liberal star took over the FTC, she was expected to break up big business. Instead, critics say, she's broken the agency.
https://nymag.com/intelligencer/2023/12/lina-khans-rough-year-running-the-federal-trade-commission.html

NLRB stretches its wings under Biden's appointees
https://www.politico.com/newsletters/weekly-shift/2022/05/09/nlrb-stretches-its-wings-under-bidens-appointees-00030967

Biden's NLRB Brings Workers' Rights Back From the Dead
https://prospect.org/labor/2023-08-28-bidens-nlrb-brings-workers-rights-back/

NLRB Guidance on Accelerated Union Election Schedule Effective at the End of December
https://www.jdsupra.com/legalnews/nlrb-guidance-on-accelerated-union-4802071/

The Union Fight for the Future of Work—and the Democratic Party
https://www.newsweek.com/2023/12/22/union-fight-future-work-democratic-party-1851297.html

Drug prices outpaced inflation since the 1990s
https://usafacts.org/articles/drug-prices-outpaced-inflation-since-the-1990s/

The Case for More Incarceration
https://www.ojp.gov/pdffiles1/Digitization/139583NCJRS.pdf

19 Companies Getting Caught Manipulating the American Free Market
https://247wallst.com/special-report/2023/06/09/19-companies-getting-caught-manipulating-the-american-free-market/

Conspiring Against Competition: Illegal Corporate Price-Fixing in the U.S. Economy
https://goodjobsfirst.org/conspiring-against-competition/

Revealed: top US corporations raising prices on Americans even as profits surge
https://www.theguardian.com/business/2022/apr/27/inflation-corporate-america-increased-prices-profits

Biden administration threatens seizure of US-funded drug patents if prices too high
https://www.msn.com/en-us/news/politics/biden-administration-threatens-seizure-of-us-funded-drug-patents-if-prices-too-high/ar-AA1l9lj8

US Tax Dollars Funded Every New Pharmaceutical in the Last Decade
https://www.ineteconomics.org/perspectives/blog/us-tax-dollars-funded-every-new-pharmaceutical-in-the-last-decade

Labor Unions in the United States
https://en.wikipedia.org/wiki/Labor_unions_in_the_United_States

In a Major Shift, Northwest Tribes — not U.S. Officials — Will Control Salmon Recovery Funds
https://www.propublica.org/article/northwest-tribes-not-us-officials-will-control-salmon-recovery-funds?taid=6584530c4d56cc00012c5cd3

Missing and Murdered Indigenous People Crisis
https://www.bia.gov/service/mmu/missing-and-murdered-indigenous-people-crisis

A radical plan for Trump's second term
https://www.axios.com/2022/07/22/trump-2025-radical-plan-second-term

What Happens Now?

For the first 80 years of the 20th century, America was on a path to realizing the ideals spelled out in the Declaration of Independence and the Constitution. Efforts to reverse the systemic discrimination that had disadvantaged so many were inexorably pushing us toward a moment when all men *were* created equal under the law, where everyone's right to life, liberty, and the pursuit of happiness was confirmed as a right, not a privilege.

That changed in 1981 and ever since then, we've been moving backward seemingly with intent toward a time when slavery was not only legal but an integral part of our economy. Not metaphorical or figurative slavery. The party of Reagan tried to rescind voting rights. They've reversed civil rights laws. They've advocated the increased monetization of healthcare and protected administrative restrictions to access it. They've dehumanized the workforce by neglecting the cost of living adjustments and abandoning the notion of a living wage. They have fought to eliminate entitlement (read: stuff you already paid for) safety nets like Medicare, Medicaid, and Social Security to privatize them and steal those funds. Have they offered how they will distribute those privatized funds? This party can't even count the votes they need to impeach a cabinet member under false pretenses, yet we're supposed to believe they can fairly distribute trillions of dollars in retirement money? They've codified the militarization of police forces and shielded the increasingly aggressive methods they've used to "enforce" increasingly draconian crime laws. They've privatized prisons and incentivized putting more people in them for lesser crimes and have increased the exploitation of the people serving... no, we're not talking about theoretical slavery, but actual, real slavery. Is this really the American Dream? Is that really what the Founders wanted?

I don't think so. They understood civilization would continue to evolve and thus that laws would need to evolve with it. They codified that belief in the Constitution with the capacity to amend it. Yet the driving force beyond the party that Reagan reshaped is a fallacy imagined by the right-wing Federalist Society (founded in 1982) called "originalism". They are a right-wing organization that advocates what they call "judicial restraint", although the way their members promote this concept can better be described as activism. Not to put too fine a point on it, but Alexander Hamilton, one of the original Federalists, argued that the Constitution did not need a Bill of Rights, that the powers and rights laid out in the Amendments were already protected by the Preamble and the first seven Articles. Anything beyond that could be decided on a case-by-case basis in the courts. What a comforting thought that we almost decided to hand our lives over to people who thought Africans were only sixty percent human, that slavery was not a violation of civil rights, that corporations are people, that business owners know what's best for their employees, that baseball is the only sport that is *not* a business, that forced sterilization is fine and eugenics is viable science, that interring an entire ethnic group of citizens in camps because they look different is fine if you're scared that all might be spies, that spending money is a form of speech, that injecting billions of dollars directly into politics won't have any measurable effects and that its OK to stop counting votes when your side is winning.

According to the Federalist marketing materials, we should interpret the Constitution the way people 250 years ago would have interpreted it. So should we only interpret the law from the same reference point as people who had no electricity or indoor plumbing, who built their own houses and made their own furniture and clothes, and who were living in a time when it took days to get information from one city to another, and all land transportation was literally horse-powered? If that really is what they intended, then any judge who is not Amish should be immediately disqualified from the bench because they would be the only candidates who understood that experience.

Reagan-appointed Antonin Scalia was one of their most outspoken members on the Supreme Court. He is largely responsible for the current interpretation of the Second Amendment, that there should be very few regulations regarding the ownership of guns. However, the first four words of that law are "A well-regulated militia". The first four... which, in the English language sentences that frequently make up our laws, often indicate they are of primary importance (unless, of course, you are Yoda). The purpose of private gun ownership was the defense of a country that had no standing army. That's not true today. We not only have a standing professional army, but we spend more on our military than the next ten highest spending nations combined, eight of whom are our allies. We spend more than twice as much on defense as our thirty NATO allies combined. Given that we've already nullified one amendment (the 18th, which outlawed the sale of alcohol), isn't it time we consider striking (or at least re-writing) another outdated amendment? Isn't it time our laws reflect the century and the country we live in? Given the absurdity of their position and their fierce opposition to the progressive policies aimed at promoting equal opportunities, there's a better argument that what they are really advocating is a return to a time when the law was written, interpreted and enforced by slave owners.

So why do people believe this Federalist nonsense? Is it because they have been spoon-fed it for decades by people who wrapped themselves in the flag and proclaimed it was good ole' American apple pie? Reagan was a big proponent of this mythology. But what he said and how he demonstrated it were often two very different things. He echoed what the Founders thought that deficit spending was bad, but then went in the opposite direction, increasing deficit spending by orders of magnitude. He echoed the Founders' contempt for taxes on the monied interests, yet simultaneously increased the tax burden on the majority of the population. Like the Founders, he said that big government was needlessly cumbersome yet expanded the federal government by 250,000 non-military personnel and increased government spending by 40% over his predecessor. Unlike the Founders, though, he had more than two hundred years of evidence that the thinking behind some of their policies needed considerable refinement, and in some cases, a complete reversal. He was like a 40-year-old man shouting like a toddler that eating ice cream every meal was the perfect diet. It sounds great, but the reality is far different. His decisions opened a Pandora's box of environmental and political catastrophes that our children, our children's children, and the generations after that will be paying for. He made our lives and their lives worse, and in some areas, far worse all the while sermonizing about the utopia of "freedom" he was creating.

His foreign policy "successes" were no better. He sermonized a pro-American vision for the world, but his tragic decision to put Marines on the ground in the middle of a Middle Eastern ethnic conflict gave inspiration to the mind that conceived and executed the most devastating terrorist attack in history. He buried us deeper in OPEC's pockets, and in the process, contributed to the further destabilization of the Middle East. He sold arms for hostages to our enemies while selling chemical weapons to a sadistic tyrant. About the best you can say is that he successfully invaded Grenada (the day after the bombing of the Marine barracks in Lebanon), but that 'success' story has more holes than a block of Swiss cheese.

Reagan's legacy includes three Republican presidents who have measurably made things worse for all but their wealthy donors, as well as two Democratic presidents who have cradled Reagan's legacy as if it was their own, perpetuating his negligence of the poor and middle classes. America is worse off ethically and economically than it was when Reagan took office, and Americans are no longer held in high esteem around the world because they have proudly been a party to their own shit show. The beginnings of the greatest transfer of wealth in the history of mankind were signaled and enacted by Ronald Wilson Reagan and his adherents.

So what was it all about? Why was it such a big deal to "defeat socialism and communism"? Because in doing so, the people who have benefited most from capitalism could point and say, "Yeah, we *could* share, but look where we'd end up if we did." So they leaned into the notion that the more unfettered capitalism is, the better it was for everyone. The evidence simply does not support that notion. In fact, given the most dire problems facing the world today, it overwhelmingly contradicts it. Economic systems, like much of life on this planet, require balance. So capitalism needs some socialism, just as Yin needs Yang, white needs black, day needs night and Spongebob needs Squidward. Both sides are necessary. The laws of equilibrium demand it.

Capitalism fosters innovation by allowing people with the talent and ambition to be rewarded for their vision. Socialism is necessary to distribute the benefit of that innovation so that all can participate in making a stronger foundation for the next innovator. It really is that simple and it's the reason why the US was so successful in the middle decades of the 20th century. Without the GI Bill, the US doesn't win the race to the moon. Without the safety nets, wealth is accumulated in the hands of the few and there is no growing middle class, proliferation of ideas, or markets for them. People would have been too worried about where their next meal was coming from, just like they are today.

A central government is simply the pooling together of resources (primarily in the form of taxes) from all its citizens to provide services to its people. When capitalists fail or refuse to provide certain services – like fire departments, infrastructure, law enforcement, public libraries, a postal service, GPS, food safety, scientific research, public education, election security, etc.

- then the government must provide them and it must do so from public funds.

The ultimate goal of the people who control the capital in a pure capitalist system is to drive down the cost of labor as much as possible so that profits are maximized. In the simplest terms, their goal is slavery. That might sound absurd in the strictest legal terms, but since the cost of caring for labor – housing, medical care, and food – under the legal definition of slavery is more than the actual wages paid for nearly 40% of the US population for whom none of those necessities are guaranteed, we're are essentially already there. Sound crazy? For a family of four, the cut-off for poverty assistance is around $30,000 per year. Add up the average monthly rent ($1372 per month), cost of health insurance ($539), transportation ($813), and food ($500 per person) and the cost just to live is over $38,000 per year. Forty percent of the population in the US makes less. As for the modern day equivalent to slaves - the prison population – the US spends an average of $45,771 per inmate per year. For many, too many, they live their lives in indentured servitude to a debt they will never be able to pay and their only crime was being alive now.

It doesn't end there. If someone graduates with a college degree, even if they have managed to do so without an encumbering debt, should they decide they aren't being compensated fairly they are far too often restricted from marketing their wares to other potential employers by non-disclosure agreements and non-compete agreements. Employers frequently hold severance packages hostage in exchange for that ransom. So to get what they are owed, many have to sign away their economic freedom temporarily. That's not slavery, obviously, but how is that not a form of indentured servitude?

So does this make Reagan and the current GOP evil for facilitating the expansion of this system? One might look to Robert Heinlein's 1941 novella Logic of Empire for insight when he wrote, "You have attributed conditions to villainy that simply result from stupidity". Robert Hanlon famously streamlined it in

1980: "Never attribute to malice that which is adequately explained by stupidity." The same as it ever was. That might have been true for the Founding Fathers with our first national experience with slavery. They did not have the will to end a practice that had been accepted all of their lives and needed the government to intervene. But that wasn't true with Reagan. He had two hundred years of history to learn from. He consciously chose to reverse the trend that had favored equality. His view of a limited government was made so popular among the wishful and wistful that no one with the power to slow it down or stop it has been willing to expend the capital to do so. Mary Shelley's view might be the most applicable. In Frankenstein, she wrote, "No man chooses evil because it is evil; he only mistakes it for happiness, the good he seeks."

Some have suggested to me that this book might not appeal to everyone because it does not come off as balanced. For this, I apologize. Not for what I have written, but that I did not write this book sooner. Our national discourse has become so twisted that even the most basic appraisal of the facts sounds like editorial. "Fair and balanced" these days comes off like interrupting a mugging by suggesting that rather than your money or your life, you simply give the mugger your cash and let him stab you in the foot. That way, at least both of you get something you wanted: he gets your money and proof that he meant business, and you get to keep your wallet. That's fair, right? So I apologize for not appearing to be "fair and balanced". Unfortunately, any honest effort to be objective given the facts is branded these days as leftist propaganda. As if somehow climate science or a man setting foot on the moon or the world being a globe are grand complicated hoaxes.

Perhaps the most troubling aspect of the Reagan legacy is that he re-invigorated the politics of our differences. He sermonized about an ideal America, but his policies discriminated against people of color, the poor, and LGBTQ. He campaigned against policies that tried to re-write the systemic biases that had disadvantaged large segments of the population for decades. He maintained that people only got rich because they worked hard and that if someone was poor it was because of their lack of effort. Never mind that nearly every study into this subject indicates that environment and family background (read: inheritance) are the overwhelming determining factors. Additionally, the number of people in the middle class has fallen by nearly 20% since 1971, while the number of people who fall under the lower income classification has increased by almost 9%. So are all those people just not working hard enough? Or is the system he re-established biased against them? He even tried to make people believe essentially that Americans were a different species of human, that they were superior simply because they were American. Nothing remotely Aryan about that, no.

Despite all that has happened since 1981, we the people are still captains of our fate. To echo something Mohandas Gandhi told the British leadership of India, if 335,000,000 Americans **refuse to cooperate** with corporate wage theft and the pernicious erosion of civil and human rights that have been driven by right-wing billionaire lobbying efforts, there is nothing the billionaires can do to stop it. Through peaceful, non-violent non-cooperation and exercising the right to vote, those who have been victimized by more than forty years of bad policy can demonstrate to them the wisdom of upholding their responsibilities to everyone else. And maybe that should be the legacy of Ronald Reagan and the presidents who followed: they were the wake-up call that our freedoms and rights are precious. They should never be taken for granted, because the moment we do, someone will find a way to profit at our expense by taking them.

The Worst Supreme Court Decisions of All Time
https://www.findlaw.com/legalblogs/supreme-court/13-worst-supreme-court-decisions-of-all-time/

How the American middle class has changed in the past five decades
https://www.pewresearch.org/short-reads/2022/04/20/how-the-american-middle-class-has-changed-in-the-past-five-decades/

Federal Poverty Level Guidelines and Chart
https://www.thebalancemoney.com/federal-poverty-level-definition-guidelines-chart-3305843

Average Rent By State
https://www.forbes.com/advisor/mortgages/average-rent-by-state/

The Average Cost of Health Insurance in 2024
https://www.moneygeek.com/insurance/health/average-cost-of-health-insurance/

Spending: How do you stack up?
https://bettermoneyhabits.bankofamerica.com/en/saving-budgeting/average-household-monthly-expenses

What Is the Average Monthly Grocery Bill for One Person?
https://www.sofi.com/learn/content/average-grocery-bill-for-1/

Do Half of Americans Make Less Than $35,000 a Year?
https://www.snopes.com/news/2023/05/17/half-americans-make-less-35000/

How much do states spend on prisons?
https://usafacts.org/articles/how-much-do-states-spend-on-prisons/

www.ingramcontent.com/pod-product-compliance
Lightning Source LLC
Chambersburg PA
CBHW011550070526
44585CB00023B/2525